To: T

Purple River

AN INSPIRATIONAL AUTOBIOGRAPHY

Thanks for your Support

Annelle J. Elder

ANNELLE JOHNSON ELDER

PURPLE RIVER BOOKS ENTERPRISE LLC

Control# 15065746

ECO Copyright 1-2545983051

LCCN # 2015953965

Let Frustration Cease

Wake up in peace, you can choose to let frustration
cease.
Say good-bye to the unwanted pain
Talk to God and try again.
Oh no it's not easy, somebody lied
there's millions of people who tried and tried.
remember the saying "sweet Bye and Bye.
Go ahead just trust him, He's by your side.
Stand tall keep walking, I'm telling you
This world better be ready,because God is using you!

Written by Author
Annelle Johnson Elder

The story of a young girl who loves the color Purple.

Her life started out in a very dark place. Living in the Arbor Hill area of upstate Albany, New York. Read this Intriguing Novel as she shares real life events and experiences meant to help other young ladies, women, and the men in our lives to better understand the importance of making wise decisions when we are younger.

Her ride on the "Purple River" taught her some things that changed her life forever! Also see how she connected with people, diagnosed with ALZHEIMER'S disease for more than two decades. I saved a seat just for you!

Annelle Johnson Elder

7/20/2015

TABLE OF CONTENTS

ACKNOWLEDGEMENTS

Thank you Lord Jesus for blessing and keeping me when I felt like the "unwanted child" throughout my life, and letting me know early that you deserve the Highest Praise!

Ms. Marguerite Johnson ("Nana") for showing me what unconditional love truly means. She gave a confused, brokenhearted little girl a chance to grow without worry in a healthy environment. Angels do exist; I will forever be grateful and try to honor the memory of my grandmother by making her proud and being the best I can be. It is because of the unselfishness of Nana, in allowing me to share her time, world, and love with me that I am what I am. I love you, Nana. Thank you for coming to visit me in my dreams with a powder pink sweater on. Saying to me with your gentle smile, "Don't forget to moisturize." This was Nana's regimen nightly, to moisturize.

Mr. Leroy A. Elder, my husband who has been better to me than my own parents, in all honesty. I have told him this on many occasions. He is my friend, lover, business partner, sounding board, and confidant and lastly, one of the most valuable gifts God blessed me with, a loving faithful husband. Thank you, my love, for walking with me through my dysfunctions and uncertainties. We are both better people individually and collectively because of our union. You proved there are good men in this world. I am happy to have one of them!

To Daddy "Ernest Victor Johnson" you opened your door to me and my baby birds (my girl's) when I relocated from N.Y to The ATL in 1987. This was bittersweet. Being honest, I will have to say the tenure at my dad & V's house brought me to tears and much pain on different levels. I still thank them both and love them both. After leaving their home, I was near to having an emotional breakdown. We've smoothed the concrete with love, respect, and forgiveness after years of my just wanting to be as far away from them as possible. Now it is a routine for us to check in on each other, mainly to say we love each other always. Not to mention the support system we have after years of being in a messy place emotionally. Daddy & V, I truly love and thank you from the bottom of my heart! Nothing like a dad who is active in the life of a young daughter to guide her heart through the world, assuring her life, will be okay. My dad is a special man in my heart for various reasons: for the funny, handsome, smart man that extended our family to the tune of having nine children (and to my eight siblings: I love all of you). The relationships were all fragile for their own reasons.

Daddy Thank you for taking your daughters and granddaughters out for lunch every Mother's Day and the money, flowers and the beautiful cards you gave us all. These are some of the attributes that make you special in my memories.

Lastly, thanks for telling me how beautiful you thought I was as a baby girl and for having a loving family that loved and kept me when you did not.

Mary Jane, I love you and thank you for, as you said, "Cleaning my soiled diapers" laughing out loud! The times I spent with you, daddy, and my sister's are etched in my heart, while remembering the time spent in California as a toddler. From me being tossed around from pillow to post often, there would be times I landed with my dad for spells throughout my life. Mary, you would sew all of our pretty little dresses with the head scarfs to match. I loved that all of us dressed alike. This was a feeling of belonging to me, to someone and something. I'm forever Thankful to you in my heart!

To Aunt Joyce & Uncle James Collazo- Aunt Joyce is my dad's sister, who has been a nurse for at least fifty or more years, she never had a daughter, so God gave her to me. Auntie would bathe me, washed my hair, grease my scalp and did my hair all the time. This was a big deal; I would know as a hairdresser. Aunt Joyce kept me when Nana worked. She would also take me clothes shopping and she would beat me too! She was my other mom; yes I was young, stubborn, hardheaded and missing the mother I never had, which caused me unthinkable pain. I say all that to make the point to thank God once more for placing me in the hands and lives of these wonderful women to love and protect me from myself. Uncle James and Aunt Joyce have been more than a blessing, to say the least. Amelia Island, where they live, is one of our favorite places, right on the beach we frequent.

To Grandma Bee "Erie Grady", my mother's mom, who was my heart and soul. I feel that a lot of my personality traits came from her and my love of cooking soul food. Thank you grandma, for also teaching me to keep my babies with me, to be a mother to my children at all times, and for that Old school love; Keeping it 100 as the youngster's say. I miss you so very much! I have to share that my soul had to recover after losing both of my grandmother's. I felt as though my support beams had collapsed from under me, even though I feel they made sure I was well-equipped to stand on my own. But from years of me being under their wings and living so close around them, I would pick up priceless jewels of wisdom from these wise women. Grandma you told me while fixing your glasses and looking me square in the eyes to "never forget where you come from." I will be sure to never lose sight of these valuable words.

This is my reason for sharing parts of my life, with hopes of possibly helping another teenage girl or young woman who may be where I was and who feels she can't make it and is feeling that the load of motherhood is too heavy to bear. Please hang in there. God has you covered. Help will come from unexpected places and your family may be some of the ones who will hurt you the deepest or love you the most. Just do not be surprised. So stay up and stay focused on improving your life, be certain to surround yourself with positive folks. Also be sure some of them are doing better than you. In the event some of these people change along the way through life, accept the blessing of God for moving these spirits out of your way and stunting your growth or you stunting theirs. Smile and keep striving for greatness! (Sending hugs from me to you, No one said it will be easy.)

To Larry & Mary Payne, my cousins: you never said no when I needed a safe and loving place to lay my head. And thank you Mary for giving me baby shower's for my babies. I'll be forever grateful for the love you shared. Breakfast was always good at the Payne's house, the awesome pancakes and fish, Mary would cook. And those giant seasoned hamburger's my cousin Larry would make. Larry, you are a great man and father. You are my brother/cousin. Thank you all for seeing something special in me and celebrating my successes in my life as you watched me try to get it right and find balance and as I stumbled through my pain on the Purple River. Although we may live far apart, you are forever near in my heart.

My girls from around the Block: leta, Rusih, Cynth, Teena and my childhood friend Retha. "My Love and Thanks also to Hat" Mek, Linda and Swuan; we are all sister's for Life.

To Dr. Delores & Bishop El, Pastor(s) Ron & Helen, and all of the counselors who helped me to sort out my feelings and grow beyond the deep-seated pain and soar beyond my wildest dreams, along with showing me a healthy way to love myself, my husband, and to learn that a happy life, and marriage is possible with hard work. You have helped to change and enrich my life. I feel like a millionaire on the inside.

To my two dear friends I had the pleasure of meeting in Georgia, Deb M. & Deb C., we go along way back like Cadillac seats (smile). After nearly thirty years of real friendship, I love and thank you both and your families!

I had to save the best for last: to my precious grandchildren and my beautiful daughter's Tierra & Tashbina, we weathered the raging storms of life together. I write and say this with the wells of my eyes filled with tears. You girls were my rocks when I didn't love myself enough to get out of abusive relationships. I did love my babies enough to look into those innocent set of eyes and knew they deserved better. I was the only one who was going to give it to them as a single young mom; in my heart I wanted a better life filled with promise for my baby girls.

Thank God I had a dream to live a better life of love, peace and happiness. I'm a firm believer that I would now be sleeping in my grave, if I had not decided to leave Albany, New York. To the ladies in my path that have shared your tears, fears, intimate struggles and valley experiences. Thank you! You know who you are. Because of you I am stronger knowing I am not alone and never have been; we as women have grown accustom to tucking our pain neatly away and taking on the she-man roles that are not ours to begin with. You are not alone, I love you all. We are not our past! Keep walking, keep trying, and keep your hearts open for real love and pampering from Mr. Right. Millionaire status can't stop the pain we have come to know from one situation or another in our lives. Lean and depend on this: when you are by yourself, you find yourself. Work on being the best you can ever be. Material items will never make one happy; however they can keep one captive mentally, while constantly pursuing the next big thing. When you reach the place of emotional tranquility, meaning balance in your life, in my opinion you have then hit the lotto. Multibillionaire status is priceless; who would trade that? Much love ladies, keep your heads up!

To Ella Mae Lawrence ("Ma") : In my heart I still feel the need to thank my mother for allowing me to share the special place in her womb, where she did initially care for me long enough for me to grace this world. Deep in my heart of hearts, I believe my mom did not abort me because she loved my dad. My version of the facts, are heart breaking when I think too long about them. In my heart I do believe my mom suffered somewhere along her life at the hands of another; I am sure she had her own tear jerking story.

Even to this day, when I visit my mother's grave, as I turn to walk away, I always shed a tear. While standing at the casket for the last glance at her face, I silently asked my mom, "Why did it have to be this way?" I did not ask to come here, but God kept me for his divine purpose. It was on my mother's death bed that she said she loved me for the first time and I was nearly forty years old. Mom also sent me a card backing up what she said to me while in ICU, and said again, in the card, "I know I've never told you but I love you." Admittedly the day my mother died is the actual day I began to live without anger; who was I going to blame? I had to keep it moving and live the best life possible! Due to all of the right and wrong reasons, some valid and other's the jury is still out on, are the reasons I may have been too hard on my girls and sometimes felt as if I loved them too much at times. I wanted so much to be what my mother wasn't to me. She wasn't a great mom. My pain was crippling for a long season. I did not know how to process my feelings properly and thought all this dysfunction was my fault, until I was determined to get and go deep for help. Counseling can and will help a person only if you're ready to get down to the business of the true core and root of the pain. I am very proud of each of my daughter's for their own special genuine love that I hold dear in my heart as their mother. It has not been easy, but it has been worth every tear. Make yourselves proud my dears. Live your lives, live your dreams, be the very best you can be. As my daughter Tee says, "UNAPOLOGETICALLY". Be mindful there is always someone watching; they will tell you later, if they have not already, how you made an impact on their life.

We all get a one-way ticket in life. Make yours count. Kisses and love always, Mommy.

To Mrs. Juliette Hill, my editor for your knowledge, patience and humor through our editing process. God led me to your door step; I know this is true because I felt safe bringing my baby in the door and I felt even better and did not have a second thought about if my manuscript was in safe hands once I left it with you. The most Ironic part of my connecting with you is your resemblance to my mother's features and I loved that aspect. Stay blessed and beautiful Mrs. Hill. Our souls are connected forever. Hugs and Kisses to you!

To Chris O'Toole @ Blue Square Writers Studio for an excellent Proofreading Job-- You are Awesome!

Thank you!

Meaning of purple | change source]

- Purple is used to represent **royalty.** It is a sign of **power, nobility,** luxury, and ambition. It shows **wealth** and **extravagance.** Purple is associated with **wisdom, dignity, independence, creativity, mystery,** and magic. Purple is a very rare color in **nature,** though the **lavender** flower is an example.

https://simple.wikipedia.org/wiki/Purple
http://en.wikipedia.org/wiki/River

A River: Definition-A river is a natural flowing watercourse, usually freshwater, flowing towards an ocean, sea, lake or another river. In some cases a river flows into the ground and become dry at the end of its course without reaching another body of water.

Purple River is the title I chose for my book because my favorite color is purple along with the meaning of a river, although I am not connecting bodies of water together; I am flowing through my life, transitioning from a girl, then a young lady, and on to a mature woman. While on my journey I was faced with many heartaches and disappointments from those I thought loved me the most, starting with my very own mother and father; crushed was not the word. I did feel my spirit was dry until another heart and hand reached for me. At that time my outlook on life was renewed with a fresh drink of refreshing self-talk, a new kind of love and ambitions moving forward on the Purple River: Once mindful of the fact that I was alone, I decided to get it together. Perhaps you may be able to understand the uncertainties and confusion a child must have felt on such an unpredictable river ride filled with pain between these lines from the accounts of my heart. Ultimately I did grab victory and success on many levels, as I flowed from one lifestyle into another and various career paths that all came together in the end, a royal testimony. What's more beautiful than a river and the color purple combined? Read the gripping story of the now multi-talented professional woman who came from a dark beginning called life. "You may call her Purple."

Disclaimer: This is a work of creative nonfiction. The events are portrayed to the best of Annelle Johnson Elder's memory. While all the stories in this book are pertaining to the journey and life of the author, she is not a professional counselor, therapist, or adviser. She is a person who has a wealth of life experiences and knows what did and did not work FOR HER and many of the steps she took to come out of the deep depression she found herself in. This book is written to give back and encourage others to make wiser choices and to live well beyond their: Past, Pains & Hurdles. Some names and identifying details have been changed to protect the privacy of the people involved. Submissions or entries within the book are the words of the named individuals themselves and have not been altered. The entries are from accounts of their own opinions and lives, not the author. Furthermore the writings are assumed to be truthful and accurate. No monetary fees were given, promised, or accepted for the entries. The Author will not be held legally responsible or liable for any claims/damages now or in the future from any person, party, company, or heirs connected with this book. Purple River-The Book

Chapter 1

A WIND BREAKER

M y name is Annelle Johnson Elder. I am a fifty-two year young black woman, entrepreneur of more than twenty-two years, wife, and mother of two enchanting and lovely adult daughters, and grandmother of two amazingly brilliant grandchildren that I adore; Bryson (9) and Kylie Renee (6).

The origin of my family meaning, my mother is from Round Pool, Arkansas and my father from Albany, New York. This is where I was born on July 22, 1963 in Albany N.Y.

From my mother's side, I have one brother; on my dad's side I have eight siblings. Some of my siblings are in Georgia, California and Schenectady N.Y.

I was raised by Nana. She is my father's mother. We resided at 36 First Street in Albany. The circumstances of how I was given to my grandmother were less than lovely. I will just put it that way for now. Whatever your age is as you are reading my book, please understand God always has a purpose in mind for each of us. In hindsight I was meant to be with Nana. Also as painful as my river ride to maturity was, it was a destined path. Kick off your shoes and relax your feet as you read accounts of the courageous, trailblazing, barefoot, flatfoot walk this girl took, if you can. This is my heart, my story, and my pain written to aid another distraught soul into peace. One winter night the temperatures outside were below zero in Albany. My mother sent me with a note to my grandmother's house asking Nana if she could baby sit me.

Nana looked at me and what I had on, which was a dress, a red wind breaker jacket, a pair of my mother's underwear pinned up on me, and no socks; I was looking like a thrown-away child. Nana took me back to where my mother was and asked if she could keep me for good and my mom wrote yes, on the other side of the note. Can you really imagine giving a child away your child with a note? Another heart-bleeding moment I recalled in my memory about my mother was a day that she was extremely angry and wanted to live her life and erase the children from her picture called life. We resided on Clinton Avenue in Albany in the upstairs apartment. Mom wanted to go out with her man. Mind you, I was also a child suffering with asthma at that particular time, and out of medicine.

I had to be about six years old or so. Ma was so ready to go party and do her thing and not look back. I was crying and trying to breathe at the same time, due to my body being in distress from the asthma attack I was going through. We lived right around the corner from her mother Grandma Bee on 76 Lark Street, who also suffered with asthma. Next thing I know my mom was dragging me on both knees to my grandmother's house, up Clinton Ave. I remember I could barely make it up the stairs from being short of breath, and at that time both of my knees were bloody and had dirt, glass, and stones in them. Still to this day, I carry those scars on both knees as a reminder of a mother that wanted to be childless. My brother was my babysitter and he is only three years my senior. Meals were what we wished for but the main dish was mayonnaise or syrup sandwiches if there was bread in the house, and sometimes we were beat for saying we were hungry.

This made my mother angry. I can also visualize some neighbors from across the street when they would come in from shopping and us looking at them as a family unit; the father was a heavy drinker, but at least he was still present for his family in my young mind. The mother of the house would give each of us a tangerine. We were nearly starving often times. Sadly even though we were hungry regularly, I thought my mother was an excellent cook that owned her own restaurants here and there. As life would have it, so many people would tell me how we stayed here, there, and everywhere, and how my mother would leave us anywhere and never was responsible to come back as she agreed to. Another incident was when my mom actually went out of town on one occasion and left me and my brother in the apartment alone; the next door neighbor heard us continually crying we were only toddlers. I was still in diapers, and a man name Mackey kicked the door down to rescue us. From all accounts my diaper was soaked to the point, when I was picked up; the diaper fell to the floor. My brother has his own traumatic stories to tell. My writings are therapeutic to say the least, with every word I type. Whenever I was old enough to remember, I just felt that this nightmare would never end. How could a mother be this horrible? However she was still the lady named Ma to me. With every painful fiber etched in my heart and soul, I whole heartedly say thank you for saying yes to Nana on the reverse side of the note. It was the best decision my mother ever made for my life. I only wished the same for my brother, who ultimately grew up in the streets and ended up spending twenty years or more in prison, and was released twenty days or so after our mother's burial. Was that another tear jerking thought or was it just me? Moving on with my life's account of the snowball madness, from the gate, my brother never had a fair chance at life. Nana always believed a child at least deserves a fair, fighting chance at life and that is what she gave me: glory!

Nana was a very sweet intelligent woman who instilled many valuable life lessons. The thing that I did not know was that my Real Estate pruning was underway and the Purple River was flowing. I would play with my doll babies, lying on the carpet, watching the Jefferson's, Mary Tyler Moore, Hee Haw, Lassie, Fat Albert and the wonderful world of Disney with Nana. The Rainbow bright doll head, my African doll Iyana and my Barbie dolls are the dolls which I learned to braid hair and apply makeup. I still love the thought of my baby dolls to this day.

As a little girl I'm thinking I had to be around eight or nine yrs. old. While living in a three-level red brick apartment building with four studio apartments above our living quarters, we did not have a cleaning lady. Therefore, I became the cleaning girl, at least trying to do the sweeping, mopping hallways and stairs, wiping down spiral wood banisters, meeting and greeting people. I have to admit, I got good at it quick. Watching and listening to Nana deal with contractors, painters, roofer's surveyors and the IRS; eventually I would come to learn a wealth of real estate, customer service and business communication skills!

Most of my time was spent watching my grandmother as she would interview prospective tenants. Over the years I noticed Nana mostly had male tenants. One I remember was Mr. B. Epps who happened to be a heavy drinker and would stumble his way up the stairs routinely to his apartment. However he was always on time paying his rent and was really respectful to Ms. Johnson, who is my Nana. As a girl looking at this man, it was hilarious to me because he was so drunk with big knots and bruises on his face from falling down. Now I look at it as sad, and I wonder: what caused him to drink to that extent? Maybe internal turmoil I'm not sure. Mr. K. Beck was a younger white guy who seemed to be special needs or maybe simply lacked good social skills. His transportation was his bike. And Mr. John, who was nice too, he was an older man. I remember his girlfriend would come often to visit with him; maybe he was a player, player? I remember his hat was always tipped to the side and he was a nice dresser. Hey, once again the most important factor was that the rent was paid promptly on the 1st of each month. Nana was reasonable when she needed to be with her tenants.

Renting to family... oh yeah, then we had my cousin Shar, a young lady probably twenty-one or something close to that age. I kind of loved it when she moved in. The Thanksgiving holiday was upon us and Shar decided to cook a turkey; I was watching her as she washed the bird and proceeded to put it in the oven. Time went by and she said "Okay, we can eat". Oh my, we cut the bird and blood ran from the meat and not only that the packaging was still inside the poor bird; by this time I was thinking maybe my cousin needs a cooking lesson or two? Nana also taught me early how to feel for the joints of a chicken and cut up a whole chicken; this talent stills saves me money at the grocery store, knowing how to cut up a chicken, instead of buying it cut up already. You may not realize that you pay extra for the precut bird at your super markets.

Today's young girls don't know anything about that. By the way, Shar didn't last long with Nana. I think I was getting old enough to understand why people try not to mix money and or business with family it is not a smart move, typically. "One size fits all" is a mindset I try to stay away from, because there are always exceptions to every rule. Thinking back about my young cousin, she was finding her way as well through life. Nana extended her hand up again for another heart in need. Nana passed away nearly seventeen plus years ago, and her memory will keep me company for life because of the love she shared and poured into me and my future. I will always strive to live a great life and make you proud. With death, we will never have any way of knowing the impact that the void of losing such a significant person in your life will have. All that I can share is that it is a feeling of such pain and emptiness. There are no words I have heard yet that ease the pain in my heart. So please cherish the special people in your life and let them know how important they are in your world now.

Chapter 2

THANK YOU FOR SAYING YES, MA

Saturdays at home were chores and run errands days. Nana was off every weekend. She worked her way up the ladder at the N. Y. Telephone Company. So we would feed the dogs and go shopping in Menands, a shopping plaza Nana and I enjoyed frequenting because it was like one-stop shopping: they had the grocery store, drug store, liquor store, and Sears Roebuck along with McDonald's. Oh, I can't forget Ted's Fish Fry a little further out in Menands, when the fish they fried hung out the bun. Simply delicious!

As we co-existed, I would hear a lot about Nana's pain in life as a young woman and mother with an abusive husband, along with her stories of coming from Virginia. The painful memories of my grandmother's life would make me cry and did trigger thoughts that caused me to relate to another human being's tragic life. However I mainly looked at her actions and how she lived her life as she unselfishly took care of me. She would spend a good amount of her time on the phone with government agencies trying to get some type of assistance for me, being that Nana gained custody of me by a handwritten note in the dead of winter. It sounds harsh, however I thank my mother now for letting Nana do what my mom could not do, and which was to be a loving mother to me.

My dad was living his life. I would see him whenever he traveled to Albany. He had another family so it was as if I had two absent parents. And people had the nerve to wonder what is wrong with this child? She acts out so badly, but they have to take ownership for their contribution to my dysfunction. It was due to the lack of love from both parents, lack of attention, and resources that the shunned child felt as the result of the broken relationship between my mom and dad. I was the ultimate loser and deprived of parents that I longed for. Going through life often wondering what did I do, and why did this happen to me, and why don't they want me? I'm their flesh and blood, I'm their child. I found the gun and contemplated suicide from the deep pain I felt and the ugly girl I saw, whenever I looked in the mirror with tears in my eyes. Looking out the bedroom window on 36 First Street in Albany is where I would have ended my life, looking out to the back yard, with a fence at the back that lead to a dirt road. On down that road was a funeral home to the right side of the road. My heart knew that was where I would lay in state one day. The gun had a safety valve, so I was spared for this season to help and save others.

Thinking back when I was in elementary school, one day I came home and Nana told me to go get the receipt book for her. She sat me down and taught me how to fill out each section of the rent receipt book. Who knew but God Almighty, what Nana was pruning me for: my real estate career as an appraiser and home inspector? Reflecting on this brokenhearted, shattered-spirit child, which had been compromised by her mother in more ways than one, The Purple River was flowing and connecting to positive thoughts and things other than the horrible pain a child should not have to experience. Life was changing for the little girl and the sun started shining. The young girl with a beautiful gap in her teeth saw a reflection in the mirror of ugliness, until a gentle hand pulled my hands down from my mouth. Whenever I smiled I would cover my mouth because I had a unique wonderful feature that I did not know or recognize as beauty or how to accept this at such a young age. The differences in people are what make the world a royal and interesting place with the variances of mankind. Thank God for variety. Can I pause for a moment to say that I can't even say how many of our own business receipt's I have written for our company, Elder's Real Estate Enterprise (est.2002) The seed was planted and nurtured routinely. Thank you, Nana. You did it and I say this with tears flowing in my heart as I write these lines. Where would I be without your helping hand that saved me from the world of struggles, loneliness, and heartbreak that I knew all too well as a child?

My childhood was not filled with all happy memories when I reflect on my parents and how grandmothers always had a way of softening the blows in life. Nana was my savior, mentor, and life coach; this is before the mainstreams of folk were dealing with life coaches. How was I suppose to understand how priceless she was, being by my side and being my protector? Truthfully she indirectly walked me into the doors of becoming a Licensed Real Estate Appraiser for the state of Georgia alongside my hubby Mr. Elder. Once I passed the six hour test, I pinched myself to make sure I was not dreaming, because I had really passed the test.

We hit the ground running to get all the knowledge we could get to become as successful as ever in our field of study. Life went on. I grew up and distanced myself from my family that nurtured me as, a child, and I went on to find myself.

Chapter 3

THE PAIN I LEARNED
TO TRUST FROM
MR. WRONGS

Prior to meeting my wonderful husband, I seemed to be drawn to unhealthy, awful, abusive relationships with men.

Remember I did not have a man or father to guide me through those tender years. No one to open car doors for me, as my husband always has and does for me and any woman in his presence. No one to carry those heavy objects into the house, or just the positive male figure that every young lady needs consistently in her view to see the strong yet gentleness that men offer and contribute to the soul of a blossoming women. Most of the inventory of men in the world I observed was cheaters, liars, absent fathers and for the most part, not to be trusted. I heard the same stories over and over again about countless men in my family that had affairs, hurting the wives, children, and themselves with criminal records, dealing with drugs, relating to using or selling illegal narcotics and domestic violence charges against women. So what kind of male figures were they? I can only truly say, it may have been just no more than three men in my entire family who were positive male figures I would look up too. While these people were labeling me a bad kid, I looked at them as bad adults, because of the actions I saw from them. My prayers are that the dads, husbands, brothers, uncles, friends, granddads and mentors will all see the vitality of their presence in our lives as women. Our pain is magnified without you there, while we put on the pretty little mask again and go on saying life is great.

Here is an instance of enduring the pain that we were pretty much blindsided with: being caught in the middle of two people who created you and for any number of reasons are divorcing or going their separate ways. As a child you are stuck, as my girls may have felt. Many times leaving can be the best scenario for all those involved. But the pain is so confusing, especially to young children, both sexes. Specifically I am referring to the daughter-father relationship at this time; it is crucial for young girls and ladies to stay connected and close to their dads, when and if the relationship is healthy. The reasons are countless of why this is necessary. The men that have remained in the lives of their daughters, I personally thank you!! This is not intended to bash, or disrespect any man including my dad. However, I am simply sharing my personal feelings and those of many, many girls and women whom I have spoken and connected with throughout my journey. Although it is never too late to step in and stay part of the picture called her life as long as you both still breathe, live, and desire such a relationship. Regardless, we need our men to own up and step up to the plate and make that lifelong commitment to stand and stay once they become dads and husbands, please? Honorable men do not abandon their families. There is a way to do all things with respect, which leaves everyone with dignity.

Dads are supposed to be our hero's. Sadly to say, a large amount of my pain came from self-inflicted wounds, once, I became grown, by constantly picking the wrong knuckleheads from the hood. You know what I'm saying? Men who were not educated who also had no goals and were abusive men. I knew I needed to aspire to rise above what I would see daily, looking out of my living room window on Second Street in Albany. My thoughts of women happily waiting on the mailman to get their food stamps and welfare checks helped me to realize this was not for me. I definitely do not want to act brand new or get it twisted; I was also a young black mother waiting on those stamps, visiting food pantries on a regular basis, expecting my Medicaid cards and welfare check, but was not happy doing so. Section 8 was a blessing in disguise, as it did allow me to press on and use the system as a stepping stone and a handout in Georgia.

Living my life in my new place was getting better, step by step. I knew this was not the end of the road for me. I said to myself, "A measly welfare check that was already spent before it came in the mail?" Hey I still miss those food stamps, I'm just keeping it 100. Food is expensive; God continues to bless me to purchase the food I want my family to have with cash honestly earned. Still to this day, I can say the best thing I did was to get out of Albany N. Y. When I hear people speak of Father Time, I can say, "He has been good to me". When I look back on the awful choices I made, being young and thinking that I had all the answers, actually I did not have a clue about womanhood, motherhood, and what a good man was. Young ladies have to stay close to their mother's or another positive female figure to guide them and show them the way through life. Whether you are a young or a mature woman, we still need awesome influences and those we can trust, love and confide in, who have weathered storms, valley experiences, and who have ridden their own Purple River rides in life in the following areas: men, children, education, health issues, divorce, being a Stepmom, money-smart, successes, failures, growing pains, losing loved ones, being victims of circumstances, sexual abuse, sexual identity, and falls from grace and living your dreams. All of these topics are vital and shape our lives as we become women.

I promise. If you have not faced any of these situations, you have not lived long enough, so hang in there! I was moving so fast, I ended up catching a case because of a bar fight. The sad thing about poor choices and not thinking rationally when you are young is that later on down the river those crazy choices we made as youngsters may bring road blocks, or hurdles as we age. I was sentenced to probation, served two days in the county jail. I felt like I had done two years seriously. You talk about crying like a baby. My poor choices of hanging in the nightclubs, with my first husband drinking and acting a fool blemished my criminal background. Most importantly I learned a hard lesson from trying to be grown too fast. I eventually picked up and relocated to a better life with greater promise. Personally, back then, I felt my children would have a great chance at life, to be exposed to cleaner and fresher air, a brighter environment, and more positive people who have changed the course of their innocent lives, not to mention mines. Leaving New York I had both hands full with a baby girl in each one. I couldn't dare leave my babies behind. That would have been worse than me staying in the madness.

This young girl was living fast, had a clouded mind of bad memories of abuse and pain. Still God kept me! If it were not from a mouth of a teenage girl, who was at that time my sister-in-law. She came to our apartment this particular day, and I had been fighting with her brother, who was my first husband. She saw how bruised my face was, one eye so large that the sunglasses would not stay straight on my face. I was packing up to relocate to Georgia; I had had enough of abusive men. God sent her to deliver me a message, this young lady said to me "I'm going to miss you and the girls", and went on to tell me I was a good mother. She advised me to "take all that negative energy you feel now and turn it into positive force when you get where you are going" we cried together. I still love her for the heartfelt message of inspiration when I needed it most. I had nothing else. Lord knows I needed all of the inspiration and encouragement I could get. From all accounts-- I will call him Tah-- this man was super handsome to me and a body to die for. I was breathless each time I saw this man. The club scene was the hotspot for me, still moving fast in the streets and getting nowhere fast! There was a club on Northern Blvd; back in the day, that was the spot. We would connect there and drink pink or green champel. We had nothing to offer the other except more dysfunction; the same tune was playing for me, going to the jail house, prisons, receiving jail calls and letters, taking my children to the prisons and jails for visits with their dads. "Child, please." I was clinging to their every word of watered-down promises from behind bars. Well this girl had enough of that grime world. Fine meant handsome, Mr. Wrongs with nothing to offer me but headaches and heartaches.

Mental and emotional abuse is what I allowed in my life because I had low self- esteem. I had to learn how to love myself and what to expect from a man. From all accounts my ex-husband doesn't have much to show for himself or his life. Such a sad thought of an able bodied man with a charming personality, which is what, got me. But ladies, please, we must look way beneath the surface to see what we are truly getting in a man or father for our children.

Oh my God, I was crazy about this man. We would dance together, go to the clubs and run in the snow. My ex-husband Tah and I were married in his mother's dining room. We were inseparable in-between the jail time and prison time; it's amazing how a person will attract the wrong thing at the wrong time, for the wrong reasons or feelings. We had one daughter; even though he loves her, he never did anything but gave me a beautiful child in which I truly want to thank both men for my precious daughters/ gifts. Here it is thirty years later and I may finally get a portion of what has been owed to me over all of these years, of raising my child alone. Feeling let down and disgusted with both of these men. I decided to go on with my life and do all I could possibly do to make sure my children had what they needed, without their father's around. Both men were totally irresponsible, straight up no chaser. Of course I was brokenhearted again! So much unbearable pressure and pain I endured as a young single mother, it did make me stronger. Both of my children were delivered via natural childbirth, moreover I also delivered my girls without their fathers by my side. What an experience. The other sad thing was these men have never understood how an absent dad leaves unsettled feelings in a young girl's heart. The void of a dad or a husband is a space no one else can ever fill. Although it may sound like an excuse, I would share with my girls their dads are not good examples for them and definitely were not good from my discretion.

Leaving Albany was giving them a true chance to blossom into the lovely flowers they are today. Their fathers will never know personally, just how articulate, chic and smart these young women are, or how giving and God-fearing their daughter's are. Especially when it comes to how much love they have shown me as their mother and helped me through some of my Purple River storms. The reason they were so willing to come to my aid is for my being the mother I have try to be and for doing the best I could from where I stood. I was not a perfect mother by any means, I do not know of one. I am more than proud of my investments in my children; they are the investments of a life time!! Lord knows I've always adored my girls. Unfortunately, I was never able to give what only a dad can give: his undying love and knowing the levels of respect to demand from a man. Gratefully my dad did share some advice that I took heed to. He said, "Take care of your children, always keep yourself up, keep your house clean, have your own things in life, etc. education, place to live, money, transportation and respect. Additionally select a man that will be good to you and for your children and do not have any more kids." Lastly, Daddy said "do not always give sex every single time your man ask, make him deserve and miss what you have to offer". Now all of the aforementioned fatherly advice I did find priceless.

Thanks daddy!

Chapter 4

HANG ON IN THERE!

"Keeping it Moving" Hello, it was my time to shine, pick up my dusty, rusty and make it happen in my new environment. When I left New York I was a heavy cigarette and weed smoker, heavy Hennessey drinker; gladly I've left those things behind me. Today I do not need anything to keep me numb, because the pain has subsided. Just to keep it real with myself and my reader's I still like to do a sippy, sip on the Mr. Hennessy and Miss Margarita or the lady named strawberry Daiquiri on occasions, socially. Come on and laugh with me while we can before the purple river shifts into another current.

Life continued to shift for me as I lived with Daddy and V, me coming from New York with two children, a high school dropout and separated from my first husband, this all meant I had a lot of hard work to do to get myself together. In the meantime, there was major stress daily. We did not see eye to eye; I hated living in their house and I felt she hated us being there too. So I would call my Nana and cry on the phone and tell her the treatment I was going through, and how I made such a huge mistake coming to their home. Nana would tell me to stick it out and she encouraged me to hang on in there and that God did not bring me this far to leave me. Mainly, she told me how she understood my pain. My dad did not believe anything I was telling him about things that would happen when he was not present. Eventually the truth was revealed, years and years later, so here it is! I was carrying more pain inside, because I was looked at as a liar. V owned her mess and I owned up to mine and daddy was in the middle of this huge pile of, well, you fill in the blank. I must admit when I lived with them in California, I would show plenty of rebellion towards her. Being honest, Ms. V has been through a lot from a man with seven other children. Without a doubt, Ms. V does deserve respect as I look back on what she has dealt with specifically from me. Starving for love and acceptance in the wrong arms was my biggest problem.

The real problem started as a child being given away. The feelings of pain followed me and did spill into my entire life. I once heard my cousin say "people have to look at where the problem originated before making or passing judgments." Self love and loving circles of people, along with allowing a place for forgiveness in my soul has helped me to repair some of those feelings from my past. God was stretching me in a good way. I didn't know how to be good to myself yet; I was busy trying to prove myself to people in the street that couldn't care less about my well-being. Thinking back, when I told Nana I was ready to leave her at the age of fifteen, I thought for sure I was grown and stubborn. She advised me that if I left her home, that was it. She was not having me in and out; she was brokenhearted with my behavior. Sadly I left, never to return, and my life changed forever. But I did finally rebound later in the game. Becoming emancipated at the age of sixteen was another great road I traveled; now I was my own mom in my mind. Fast forwarding, I had a baby within a couple of years of leaving Nana, from my first abusive relationship from this young man that was just as mixed up as myself. Then I started again, running to prisons and jails visiting him, putting my little welfare money on his books; man was I fool in love.

Well I got pregnant at seventeen and had my daughter T at seventeen. Child support was just a dream for my baby: I have shared with my girls, I feel like I've stood in every line there was to keep my children warm, the lights on, keep their bottles full and food on their plates, and clean diapers and clothes on their backs. I was so broke that the cloth diapers were good and bad: it was nice to put quality cotton diapers on the babies but who wanted to wash those stank, soiled diapers? I did not, but no one else was there to help me pull the slack. You talk about growing up fast, now I did not have a choice. And I married my first husband who was just as bad as the first guy; I was batting a thousand with Mr. Wrongs; what was my problem? My family was afraid that we were going to end up killing one another from so much fighting. Domestic violence is not just physical; it can be emotional, mental, and social. It leaves deep mental and emotional scares.

The first guy-- I will call him G-- was a person that was so full of his own pain that all he knew was what he was filled with: confusion, anger, alcohol and drugs.

It took me time to grow up and learn that we can't give away what we don't rightfully own ourselves, especially love. The man G was terribly violent; he left me with fear and deliberate pain in my soul. I was always afraid he would try to truly hunt me down when I left New York and kill me, or I would have killed him in self-defense. He was so very mean, although he loved his daughter T but did not do a darn thing for her. Time has a way of showing us how messed up we really were in different seasons of our lives. A good thing about the Purple River is it keeps on flowing. To see clear is a blessing within itself; this can also be devastating to say the least, when you see how you actually allowed such craziness to consume your time, life, and energy from people which did not deserve to share your space in the first place. Hind sight is 20/20; please believe it! Oh yeah the guy G, he is still feeling some kind of way about your girl, meaning me. He constantly asks what I'm doing? What kind of car am I driving? Now I have a question? What difference does any of that make to the man who did not know how to treat me as a seventeen year old young girl, looking for love in all the wrong places? One of those places was in his arms... wrong move? Far as I was concerned, maybe it would be great for him to figure out how to remove the concrete blocks from his heart and mind. Nana always knew I was a diamond in the rough. I had bigger fish to fry in getting my feet wet in this place called A.T.L Hot Lanta, yes! I made it out.

Albany is where I was born and bred. The streets of Arbor Hill taught me lessons that books could not. For many reasons, I felt I needed to share some of my life, in hopes that another young girl or lady may read my struggles and possibly think twice, prior to making poor, life- altering decisions. Clearly always stay mindful of whom you seek council from, be sure to observe their life, and see if the person appears to be standing on solid ground first, mentally and emotionally before you lean to heavily on their advice. Keep in mind that material things DO NOT make them a role model. More so, just because a person is a family member does not totally make them a role model either. All I can say is "Do your research." Throw your hands up! I am on a roll now. We are moving forward!

Chapter 5

MY GIRLS, BOOKS AND BOYS

The girls were ages five and one when we relocated to Atlanta. Now those same precious girls are thirty-four and thirty years old. They are on their own journeys. As a mother of two children I have shared some very painful places with my girls; watching my girls go through relationship situations less than attractive, I am standing by watching my oldest child juggle being a women, wife, mother, graduate of UGA, entrepreneur, homeowner, and a self-published author; all of the aforementioned titles can come with a lot.

You are doing an amazing job Tee, remember I am your biggest fan; our relationship has been through the test of time. We are two strong personalities that stayed in the battle field, our spirits clashed so many times I have lost count. With love on the front page, and because love was always in our storms, we continue to love and bless each other as only the Mother and daughter relationship does for the God-given two people. It is not ever easy to watch your child dive off a cliff; so to speak, when all we can do as parents who are present in the lives of our children is to warn them of the consequences that will typically follow certain decision they make when they are young. Once you've counseled them first, I just tried to catch them if, and as they land as someone did me. My other child is just as sweet as the first child. A very sensitive soul that God allowed to be born the same day as Nana, January 6th, this child was my road dog; I say it with smiles. She always wanted to hang under her mommy. We were out in a rainstorm driving around, looking for a house to purchase and we found our house-- it was actually two places for sale on each corner. We liked the house to the right: it was a pretty brick dwelling with a full basement and large beautiful yard, front back and sides, and seemed to be large enough for us all.

Anyway my baby girl grew up and did well in school. She has taken many college classes, mentors young ladies to this day, is a self- published author; she also has plenty of experience in her field of selling upscale jewelry. She has shed her share of tears as well because of picking Mr. Wrongs. Sadly she came close to taking her own life, out of desperation and lack of self-love at that season in her life. God kept her for the world, to liveout the purpose he created her for, as she helps and saves others along her journey. Her testimony is undoubtedly a tear jerker, especially for the person sitting in the seat for Mom. The world held my child in its hands until God released the grip. My child walked through the darkness she chose and came out on the winning side, alive. Glory to God! Regardless of the season she was in, my love never wavered for her. I know without a doubt God does hear a mother's prayer. Some of the pains my children felt I shared with them for other reasons; as a mom we always feel like we could or should have done more and said this or said that. We have to stop being so darn hard on ourselves! We are one heart, one body, and one soul, spreading our love in what seems to be a million places, trying to save everyone but ourselves. Today I still cheer my girls on from the side- lines of their lives, but will have no problem checking them at the door if need be as well, when they need a word that sometimes only a mother can give. I do try to keep that check in my pocket for the most part. They are women and I do respect their positions. In fact, I feel I have given my daughters a loving foundation that was not perfect, however that was stable with more love than money always.

Eventually after moving from apartment to apartment, we moved into a very cute section 8 house with a purple crape myrtle tree blooming in the front yard near the mailbox, since it was the spring of the year, when we moved there. We were transitioning and shifting upward and it felt great! The girls seemed happier, stable with friends of all nationalities who would play in our yard daily. Their friends loved to sample the fried chicken I would be cooking for dinner, for my babies. Yes I was a young mom; even though times were difficult, however, once all resources were flowing properly, we were living decent to be on our own.

A good home cooked meal was a daily routine for me; my girls rarely ate sandwiches growing up. Despite how my mother did not see the importance of having balanced meals for her children as a necessity, I did. Namely fresh greens, macaroni and cheese, fried chicken and dessert. Sometimes the kids would bake cakes, cookies or cupcakes when they were bigger. We loved living in our new place. Section 8 was a blessing in disguise, as it did allow me to press on and use the system as a stepping stone and a hand up in Georgia. Living my life in my new place was getting better, step by step. Moving forward I found out it is okay to save some love and peace for myself and that it is also okay to say no. I do love the two letter word no; I cannot save the world, without saving and protecting the best of myself first! We all have stories of pain. However it seems when we are overwhelmed we make poor choices. I have learned when I am restless in my spirit that I should first pray then talk it out, take some things or folks off of my plate and if need be, make that change towards inner peace, joy, and happiness. I am worthy to be set free. Fast forwarding my life and getting down to business with my education.

Mind you I was still in a bad place mentally with men. I got to the point of being sick and tired of being sick and tired and I had to shift into an unfamiliar territory. One day I decided to pick up my biscuits and visit DeKalb Technical College to get my process started for Cosmetology in human services. The course was nearly a two year course. I finished the course graduating top of my class, including representing the school and touring around to various other schools with the Dean of the school for career day to speak with youngsters interested in becoming Stylist or barbers. I was now a Master Cosmetologist. While I was in school I worked part time as a medical secretary in the nursing home at DeKalb Medical Center hospital. Consequently I worked the nursing home for 8 years at the hospital, truly learning people skills and public relations as well as time management. (Even though I was already good with time management, being a single mother.) Nonetheless I remained mindful to make sure the kids were, loved, fed, and cared for, off to school on time always, and to all events on time by walking them there or taking public transportation.

Chapter 6

TORN UP FROM THE FLOOR UP

At this moment I am actually very upset with myself, because I've wasted many years and precious time, really feeling the need to help other people heal, when I needed the healing myself. More than that, I needed to get over the broken men I was drawn to because they said the right thing and looked a certain way-- how wrong I was! Recently I've reached a place mentally, maybe last year sometime, of Purple Freedom while riding my Purple River.

Self talk had me going in deep to my core, taking serious self inventory and asking, "What is my problem?" God has all of his children on a path to freedom and I guess that day I found mine. The reason I felt disappointed in myself was because I'm thinking of the people that were not worthy of my energy. For unknown reasons I was trying to impress, embrace, convince, restore, encourage, inspire, enlighten and persuade folk who could care less about figuring out what was wrong with or trying to fix themselves. But no, here I come. What is wrong? Instead of working on me, who was surely torn up from the floor up, emotionally Yup, I'm being so real and transparent. I've always had a strong will, whether it was for the right or wrong reasons. The mask I wore may have come as a defense to save the little bit of dignity I manage to keep for later down the river. There were a few strong ladies who always made me feel I was worthy to live and be loved unconditionally; my heart say's thank you to them for that! No kidding. Something hit me and whispered: it is your time.

Being released from what I thought were my duties to mankind, I was even expecting and allowing other's to validate me. I'm glad the job is over because guess what? I can live now on my terms enjoying an uncluttered mind, heart and soul I had to say it was okay, not to be with those I felt I needed to be with and embrace God's will for me. Now because of the sweet release I feel, it's fine when I can't figure everything out in a split second, or if I just don't feel like saving the world today. Those people that are living the lives they desire, somewhere along the way they said the same thing to themselves. I salute them too! Possibly the heart given to me was yearning for the same thing I was trying to give and had, but didn't want it from the person offering it to me at the time. Did you catch all that? Well it sounds funny, but it is true. We are human and try to compensate for the things we don't have, what may be even worse is trying to overcompensate. One of the best blessings ever is to see my adult daughter's live life on their terms and standing on their own two feet. Please don't get it twisted, they are not perfect and don't need to be. They are young, beautiful, smart, hard-working and independent, mainly God-fearing young ladies with all of the aforementioned attributes. They may stumble in the path called life but I know they are conquerors and will be just fine. Momma laid the foundation of love, education, and hard work for them. Those of you who are waiting on hand outs will be waiting a while, because most hard-working folk will give and give but the giving will stop eventually. We all have to make our own way in this world. To be honest, when those who love us say "no", this is what we need to hear. You've heard about that thing called tough Love? I feel it works and makes us better people. Hard work can be hard, but integrity is built from that, and maturity and ethics are established. Now, on the flip side of that, if a person doesn't work, is just plain lazy, and hand is constantly out, pretty soon most people will be going in another direction.

We work hard to enjoy some of life's pleasures: trips, your own address, nice things, education along with a few luxuries here and there. My point is you don't have to ask or explain when you can handle your own thing. When a woman is like a leach or looking for a sponsor, the man will eventually lose interest and respect for that woman, due to him wanting a help mate at some point. A real good man needs a real good woman in his corner. Even if he has a side chick, he will always remember the round the way filet, meaning the real deal lady that stands alone in a special designated place in his heart. He loves her because she loves him and herself enough to bring, love, respect and contributions to the table. Most importantly as women we have to always know and love our worth. In fact one should keep it moving when we feel we are not happy and realistically see no true value in holding on to your man. Typically all hope is gone when love is gone. My grandmother's were no joke, I'm serious. They stood their ground and handled their business, with or without a man. However I was smart enough to know every woman needs a man, if they are honest with themselves, but they would not settle for the knuckleheads that didn't want to self invest.

Chapter 7

LEARNING IN THE
MIDDLE OF IT

Of course when we reach a certain age, we think we have all the answers. What I am about to share in this particular chapter may be my favorite part of the book as far as I am concerned. More so, I think this is also the longest chapter. The most valuable lessons in my life seemed to be learned in the middle of the lesson itself. Well, I will start with what I thought was just time in the day simply passing by. when I would go visit my Grandma Bee, we always sat on the stairs with my grandmother at 76 Lark Street, as I repeated what seemed like a million and one times. Little did I know this time would be some of the most precious moments ever spent! The laughs, the hugs, the cries, the wisdom, the drinks, the great family moments of my aunts, uncles, cousins, mom, friends and, neighbors, and strangers that became friends, And from time to time would frequently share those same stairs, not realizing every time I climbed the steep blue stairs on 76 N. Lark Street, God was sending me up for another major life lesson from my girl Grandma Bee. She taught me how to laugh, cook, and be a good old school mother and how to be strong. Also I learned lessons about when you have a good man, how to love people and the importance of family. Also who was and wasn't a fool, and as she put it, people that were "Crazy as a Road Lizard". Another one of my favorite sayings from my grandma was when she felt that a person was lazy or sorry in the respect of not being highly motivated, she would say, "They were not worth two dead flies riding or walking" Oh my God, I would laugh so hard nearly spitting out what was in my mouth. My Grandmother was hilarious! That is why I still miss her to this very moment and now who do I turn to when I need love?

Those front porch talks were priceless. No matter what season it was, it was always spring to me because spring is the time of the year we watch beauty unfold and blossom. I was doing exactly that. This is where I would get checked at the door, meaning get told off when I was not doing the right things due to being a young inexperienced mother ignorant to life and being immature. Or I may think I know it all because I was a legal women in the eyes of the law but truly inexperienced when it came to life and how to make it. Grandma also saved my life many times literally, by sharing her asthma pills/ pump with me to soothe my lungs while I was in the middle of severe asthma attacks. How can a thank you cover that bill?

I have never laughed so hard in all my life as I would laugh on those blue stairs with my family, almost peeing my pants many times. The quality time spent with my uncles and friends on those same steps, nearly losing my breath so many times, from good old fashion laughter. Thinking back on how I would hold my stomach because it would be hurting from laughing so hard and at the same time, tears running from my eyes.(I miss those times with my uncles, they were like my brothers; Mike, Trace and Ha.) Life has changed drastically from that era in time. This was a safe place for all of the family, especially me and the girls. I guess that is why I loved going there. The family connection meeting place was at Grandma's house on 76 N. Lark Street. Watching Grandma work magic with her arthritic hands, she would make some of the best meals I could only dream of. Real Country cooking!

Today I still try to duplicate her meals the best I can. This is my point: we don't always have to be making a million dollars or flying off to the most fabulous place in the world. The simple things in life are the best favor God has blessed me with. Recently I lost a dear uncle and the wife he left to cherish his memory after sixty-one years of marriage. She looked at my husband and I, saying, "You both have the most important things in life at this very moment, and that is each other." She went on to share, "The things don't matter." She wanted to be certain we left with her profound message in our hearts and we got her message. This was my Grandma Bee's sister, Aunt Mary (love you!) I have another aunt who looks so similar to my mom. She is my aunt T and she loves to dress up-thanks for all the lovely purses and expensive

perfumes aunt T-! I send kisses to you. Then my other aunt Tee-
- she has passed away also-- Well, she shared her lemon/vanilla
pound cake recipe with me prior to her death; this was only after
she had made these cakes for me so many times whenever I would
visit Albany. Grandma had two other sisters. Even though I never
had the pleasure of spending time with my auntie's, I do remember
overhearing grandma and aunt Ada sitting outside on Lark Street
on the side of the house in some lawn chairs one summer, just
chewing the fat, and I heard my aunt Ada say, "Bee, look at that
pretty willow over yonder." I did not have a clue of what they were
speaking about, until I kept listening-- as they call it, I also kept
ear hustling, too-- and I discovered they were talking about the
beautiful Weeping Willow tree. Because of my aunt Ada, I always
think of her when I see a Weeping Willow blowing in the wind.

God knows my aunties are special, just because of who they are.
Aunt Addie, I didn't forget you. I enjoyed spending time with my
cousins, your daughters while visiting Michigan this past summer.
May all of my love ones that have gone on rest in peace! Back to
Aunt Tee, she always sent me back to GA with a delicious smelling
& tasting pound cake. Fast forwarding to "The family cookout the
summer of 2015" and time spent in Kalamazoo, Michigan was
special for sure! There is another one of my aunties' in St. Louis,
my Aunt Mat who taught me some serious lessons in her kitchen.

Thanks Aunt Mat for that mustard greens with cabbage and aged
hocks recipe; you don't know how much I've cooked that since I
left St. Louis. Our visit to Michigan with you and the family as

we were preparing, to say good bye to my great-grandmother and your mother, whom I was named after. How was I to know the significance of these precious moments, while I was learning in the middle of it?

Growing up and looking back on hind sight and what quality family time means and its worth are sobering. Actually it is history whenever we break bread, love and hug each other, no matter the occasion. Some of the memories I keep tucked away are for instance, when I had an idea to make extra money as a young single mom. Well, I have always enjoyed cooking. Therefore I decided to prepare chitterling dinners, a complete soul food plate, collards, potato salad, cornbread, soda, and lemon cake. I worked part-time and many of the co-workers at the hospital were my best customers. I worked eight years as a medical secretary. The chitterling plate sales did so well, I pleasantly surprised myself.

For some strange reason, many people I know tell me "oh no, I don't eat that." Well, I had so many orders for my chitterling dinner plates that I ran out of the main dish. Grateful wasn't the word. My earnings were pretty good. Meanwhile I went on to clean up and rest up from such a busy day in the kitchen taking orders. Again the lessons I learned in the middle of this was my daughter's were watching me try to do the best I could alone. Also I truly think this set an example and planted a seed, that you can make it if you try. The girls saw how much money I earned and it made them want to be little entrepreneurs. My girls loved the action of that day, all the phone calls, helping mommy bag the dinners, and getting little tips for helping out; they were my extra set of legs. We had each other. Thinking back we always had decent furnishings in our apartments because I made sure we had what we needed. Time revealed the most important factor to us, and that was to love and depend on each other. I learned that valuable lesson in the middle of our small kitchenette on Austin Drive, in Decatur. Small gestures like a just because card in the mail, or a flower picked spontaneously for you to smell. There are times when a person may not be able to afford expensive gifts, but in their hearts they would love to give you something elaborate. Again, there may be times when money is not the issue.

It's just the thought that means everything! There are countless ways someone can make you feel so special that I can not name them all. You will understand as you ride the Purple River in life. And for those that understand, I need to say no more on that topic. My girls have given me my flowers and I want them to know their love will last forever in my heart. They have also given me my parental report card and, guess what, I passed the class!! Since I gave the best I could from where I stood, yes, my children saw our struggles. They also saw how we made it through some extremely tough times together. Maybe the times didn't appear that rough to the children because I bared the brunt of the storms, as parents are expected to do, as I cried myself to sleep many a nights and praying as they slept, for God to continue to help me to do better each day and help me to care for my children. He heard and answered my prayers.

My nights are now peaceful and my days are what I make them and what God sends my way. I'm fine with all three.

My heart is guiding me through this writing process; as a young mother, I would be so overwhelmed at times and not know what to do or who to turn to. This is for the young lady that feels Isolated; I say you are not alone. Please ask for help and keep praying and trying, your break through is closer than you can imagine.

Furthermore, I am still learning in the middle off it. I think back on how it may have been changing time for the baby and I would be loving on my babies and caring for them while, for instance, I may be changing their diapers. The moments spent doing this routine assignment was actually our bonding time for me and the baby. When the baby grabs your finger, testing its own strength, or when the baby looks directly in your eyes and smiles at me (mommy), that melted my heart each and every time. The smile the baby had when I would pick them up from daycare, school or even now show up just because. These are still priceless moments because I know they are happy I could make it to the special occasion. Life is so unstructured when it comes to really understanding when and what a life lesson is.

We have to catch these beautiful moments while we are in the middle of them. I am sharing this with someone or everyone who may not have a clue of what real memories of a family entails. In fact they are laughs, catching up with the family, sharing family recipes and favorite dishes, talking about each other, that happens in all families, the off springs playing with their cousins and learning how God spreads those family genes wide and far along the Purple River. When a family function is happening and someone looks around the room and so many people look alike, or the traits we pick up because of the bloodline, such as the beautiful gap in my front teeth that my grandmother, aunts and my mother all have. Consequently, my aunt is dead and gone now, but we looked so much alike that her husband thought that I was her one day on Clinton Avenue; we shared many characteristics too! I miss her and love her, R.I.P. Sugar. Family is what kept me when I couldn't keep myself. Friends are a blessing, however NOTHING compares to the love of our families.

Everyone needs a friend, those girlfriend times are a must if you want to remain sane. A real friend listens well, understands, and cares when you are in a place of pain, confusion and hardship. True friends can also give you interesting views on life, which you may have never thought of. Both of the ladies I call my friends basically we only see each other a couple to a few times annually and I have grown to love this, because it has revealed that a person does not have to be on the phone with you every day, hanging in your house weekly, or does not need to know all of your business to be considered a friend. Real friends pick up where they leave off and that is with love and respect. Holidays are typically the special times we all get together and catch up. Or periodically throughout the year, just because it is time to connect and share, or vent and treat each other with special gifts and special times for laughs. Sometime we do not understand the love and grace that we have directly under our fingertips.

Another instance of learning in the middle of it, was when Nana would make the best peach cobblers, meatloaf sandwiches and the best stacked high BLTs this side of heaven. This little girl that loved the color purple did not know that all of the quality lessons I was taught-- like 'wash your furniture with vinegar and water,' 'look a person directly in the eyes when you speak to that person.' ' be honest and loving even though you have been mistreated by family and others that claimed they love you', and 'do not be bitter, but instead keep climbing up life's ladder.' Also how you can be torn down because of jealousy and misunderstandings from people who really don't know your journey of pain, but felt they were the authority and just put negative rumors out about you, when the ones they never shared about themselves probably are worse than yours. Hum. My Nana struggled but she lived with dignity and she brought me with her and taught me how to act like a young lady, cross my legs, dress appropriately and speak with class, she instilled in me how education was the key to success. She knew my pain was more than 6 feet deep, and I knew even though I was young, she was my comforter. I will always love my Nana.

I learned how much my Nana meant in the middle of my learning to be a mother, all the time she spent praying with me, pulling me by the ear and saying get your butt up and rewash these greasy dishes, making me do my chores. In addition discipline made me a better woman. I know how important it is to take care of myself, my house, and my man, Okay, I told you I am keeping it 100 with you all. For those of you that are old enough to date, this information may be something you can identify with. Relationships can be complicating so, take your time and do not rush into dating. So far I hope that you feel my transparency and realize, I am sharing from my heart in honesty. Nana showed me how to take care of and keep a clean house and how to keep myself neat and clean, but I had to learn on my own how to get and keep a man. Can I get an Amen from somebody? There are times in life we must walk alone. I know how to do all of those things now.

On to my aunt Joyce… she was not having any of it from me. She was the eyes and ears for Nana. Auntie watched me and typically was my caregiver. I would look at her and say she is always switching when she walks and she still does today. Sometimes I guess that is where I get it from, or maybe it's automatic. Auntie has been a nurse forever it seems like. I think it is nearing fifty years or more. Auntie, thank you for your love and care. Even the morning of September 01, 2015 the day my Pre-Order's started for my book; of course this was an important day! you were the first one to call and alert me that my PayPal button was not working for my Purple River book sales. Of course I corrected that immediately! Needless to say Auntie was the first person to Pre-Order "Purple River" the Book. There are countless reasons I continue to say thank you!

All of the things you would share with me did not fall on deaf ears. I have always respected and loved the ground you walked on because again, you cared for me when I did not know how to care for myself. You were the one who pierced my ears with a needle, thread, ice and a potato (smile). I did not forget that, because I screamed like crazy down on Pearl Street. Just like I remembered how pretty I looked all the time. Y'all love me auntie and I don't know how a person really thanks the one who does all that. Your husband has also given me a lot to think about down through the years as he watched me grow up. He has often told me, "Le is the best thing that ever happened to me, I do agree." The hand up you and my uncle James extended will always be appreciated; you both knew we were going through a hard patch in life due to the real estate bubble busting and the Historical Recession/Great Depression which turned the world upside down. The love you both shared helped us to hang on in there just a little while longer.

Again I learned the lessons in the middle of growing through life. The lesson I took from my auntie was: things are not always what they seem to be. Auntie looked so mean all the time to me, but this was her way of keeping me in line. She is good as her weight in gold. Anyone who knows me knows I love gold; they opened their home, hearts, and pocket books when I needed them the most. As a result of my Nana, along with others that loved me through the hardest ride of my life. I understand life better through the love they shared.

This is why I feel the need to give back to others, going through the Purple River ride in life. Please understand: at times we will have to doc the vessel and allow another heart to board – Hallelujah!

My Christmases were wonderful because I was the only little girl around the house while living with Nana; therefore I was pampered and spoiled by you both. The summer vacations as a child were fun on the Beach of Amelia Island; I was visiting beautiful Islands as a girl, eating all of the fresh water seafood right out of the Atlantic Ocean into the frying pan. Those were the days! Thanks for being my mom for such a long season in my life. In life I have always heard how important it is to give back; you have done that with me, our family, and your patients. I know you will be wearing the nursing crown for angels. Many kisses to you Auntie. I love you more than you will ever know!!

One of the last lessons I want to share that I learned in the chapter Middle of It, is about men. A man can make you want to love him and have your head swimming. Then again a man can have you feeling like you will be just fine, if you never see another one for a good while. Either way it goes, when a woman picks a man she has to be more than careful, especially if she wants longevity, honesty and respect. And especially to be loved like a queen and to be made to feel as if his heart belongs to her only.

Yes it is slim pickings out there and it really does take time to find a good man. Be certain of what you ask God for in a man, because He just may give you exactly what you ask for. Every woman has her own description of a good man, depending on her age and needs-- emotionally, physically, financially and sexually. My journey with men wasn't the best. Ultimately I did land on my feet and regained my balance in this department. Contrary to my past poor choices in men, my loving husband is what God saved for me as I grew up and became ready for a sweet gentleman.

Was I a Diamond or a Cubic Zirconium?

Again after dealing with the lack of self love and the lack of maturity of knowing that a woman should always be treated like a diamond. The cost I paid to learn this lesson was expensive, but I paid that price. Now I know without a doubt, I am a true God-made Purple Diamond. We all have to be made a fool of once, twice, or maybe even more times than that until we get the clear message. To wake up and be self-sufficient, love ourselves, and not to be desperate for the first thing that you think you see in a man. Moreover to realize that it is so much more to this person that you don't see yet, and nothing but time spent with that person will reveal who and what you are clearly dealing with. Ask God for want you want in a man and be real to the core. Be mindful, you will get what you ask for, so do yourself justice. We all have a wish list of what we think we want. Glory to God for always sending us what we need! Therefore we may actually push a good man away because we have not matured enough yet to see the forest for the trees. Make the man date you and respect you.

Sex does not have to take place within the first month or two. As a matter of fact, sex should wait a long while. Friendship is not like it used to be. Times have definitely changed and the pressure is on, but it does not matter: a man is still a man and wants what he wants. What sets a real man apart from a dog is his approach to us as women. Some men are truly seeking friendship within the love they so desire as we do. Please, please don't say that all men are no good, wrong! Men are beautiful for our souls, especially when you happen to be blessed with a good man.

A good man is Priceless! So make him wait on the prize, if you know what I mean. Relationships are very complexed and time-consuming, even being very distracting mentally and emotionally. I mean, there are also some men who eventually turn into good men from all of the mistakes from their past. Be sure you are ready for a relationship. Oh yeah, I need to share this too: the makeup, jewels, money, the clothes, houses, fine automobiles and other material things that have us twisted in life will not bring you true love. Only a heart can attract another heart that's ready for love not lust. This world will chew you up and spit you out. Arm yourself with all of the things that will last and that will help you stand in the raging storms of the Purple River when the storms of life start raging. They are on the way, trust and believe your girl.

Here is another vital point worth considering when you are a women or a man who already has a child or children. It is totally different when dating because you are also trying to get a feel if this person will be good with you and your child/ children. My checklist was pretty long as far as what things I had to consider for my children's sake. So take your time, take self-inventory, reach some of your own personal goals first, have fun, travel, get educated, stack your paper and do not settle for less than you deserve. Additionally be sure the standards you set are realistic and you fit inside of what you expect from him or her. Be real transparent to the prospect and save yourself the precious time of playing mind games. My man is not perfect by far; the good news is I feel that I can trust him, if he is in or out of my presence. He loves the Lord and respects himself, our marriage, and all that we have worked for together.

Honestly I feel I have one of those rare husbands who has never cheated on me. I could be wrong, I'm saying how my heart feels. Just as your hearts gives a indicator your man is cheating, yes, my heart has given me the indicator that it's all good in my hood where love lives in and out of my bedroom!. Oh my God, that feels wonderful to say. I am so content in my mental space that I am thrilled with my life now. No one has handed me anything.

I have worked very hard, raised my children the old school way, moreso I have been in a long marriage filled with love, hard times and challenging times. I've prayed and kept the faith, even though I thought it was getting to hard to hang on in there. I did hang on, and God blessed me for being diligent. Hey who wants to go through rough times? I'm really being honest right now. Marriage is just as hard as raising a child or children; I compared the two because they are both very entrenching emotionally and can or will wear you slam out. We did hang on through our droughts and valley experiences because of the love and friendship we carried in our hearts for one another. God favored us for being committed and diligent in our marriage. I don't think it gets too much better than that as far as I'm concerned.

All women have a dream of what a happy life would be. Coming from the place I started in life changed my perception greatly. Considering all things, I made a good choice in my new kind of guy and I thank him for the love we share. My husband has helped me become a better person, a better mother, and better friend. I am now walking through life with a man that knows more than the latest dance moves, the latest and greatest street slang and knows a lot about hard work, a lot about fixing cars, fixing things in the house, and cutting a beautifully manicured yard. The new guy knows when to appreciate a real meal made from love and how important it is to bring his paycheck home to momma. He was needed and loved for being his gentle country self. He is the new guy that taught me new things about insurance policies, electronics, politics, patience and science. We have our days as a married couple that are not always the best, but who doesn't? He also opened up and shared his pain and insecurities as a black man, being a man within his family that carried a heavy load as well. God still stepped in and saved us both and called us closer to him; my heart is full of gratitude and tears.

Surely, I had many, many fears of can I trust what I am seeing as real love? Yes, finally a man with real interest, I mean really refreshing to talk about something other than gossip and the club. We had our times when life was not easy but through it all, I knew you were a good man, and I knew you did not want to walk away from me but walk beside me, my love. The gap in my teeth that I was always insecure about, you spotlighted and told me how pretty it is. And how beautiful your wife is, with all my curviness, and how you did your best to take care of your family and household the honest way. Because we were living and trying to do things the honest way, life got rough; but we got rougher and tougher and grew closer together. You have my deepest respect period. Life put these broken hearts together to blend and mend each other's pain openly and honestly over these twenty six years. The lesson I learned in the middle of it is that when you see married couples who weathered the storms, you need to salute these woman and men for staying and standing. There are people that will always say, honey child, after what he did I would not even take him or her back. Well we are all human first, and capable of error at anytime. Have we forgotten that no one is perfect? Commitments are not to be taken lightly, therefore when we commit ourselves we have to prioritize the commitment at all times 365, 24/7, while keeping the lines of communications open and love leading each chapter.

Get the help you need if you come to the place of feeling like you are on the crazy merry-go-round with your man or woman. Nothing is wrong with reaching out to others when you feel you need to. It is just to make sure you are listening to the right people that have your best interest at heart. "Remember everyone is not saying the same prayer for you", as a peer shared with me years ago. The lessons I learned, as you can see, are worth Gold. I think I passed the test. Don't let life and people trip you up with irrelevant opinions that don't matter anymore, because you have gotten yourself together and don't need to hang on their every word like you used to do because your self-esteem had not arrived yet. Salute yourself right now, if you made it through your Purple River storm or are still standing in the storm and still keeping it moving. Your rainbow of triumph is closer than you imagine; walk it out!

Chapter 8

GENTLENESS OF A CG=COUNTRY GUY

While I was in trade school and living in that cute house I told you about earlier, I met a guy one evening when some of my friends and I stopped at the phone booth on Memorial Dr and Covington Hwy at the Shell gas station. You know this was prior to the cell phone age. Sadly one of my friends passed away from HIV; I miss his memory as I write about that time in my life. Another friend from that era, from all accounts, Tavia, is really riding the spiritual wave now-- wonderful for her , nothing like getting a personal relationship with our Lord and Savior, Jesus Christ. One day I was on the rear deck of my cute section 8 house, studying with my head deep into my books; the girls were in school. Le was en route to the house, and this is the new kind of guy. My soul needed the country guy. Anyhow I was in the midst of a serious conversation with God as I thought about how far God had brought this seventeen-year-old girl with a bag and heart full of disappointment, low self esteem, (if any), scattered dreams, a failed marriage, and two beautiful children for whom I had to set an example for. People were in my ear, yelling, you will not make it. You left Albany, but you will be back."Once again time and events had me standing in a place in life where I had to look myself square up in the face, stop the pity party, put as they say, my big girl panties on and reinvent this young woman on a mission. As I was saying, about this new type of guy I guess real country means not cool, not disrespectful, or crazy acting. I must say he was crazy about your girl, he did not drink or smoke weed nor cigarettes, and he was always neat and clean-- never ever said a curse word except one time 'hell' slipped out. I'll take one for the team. We laughed so hard; he said, "You see what you made me do?" We laughed some more.

He did not have a rough edge; he was kind and gentle. Oh my, I had to get used to this type of man. Did I feel I deserved this man or was I use to be being treated like less than a lady? This man made me check myself without him telling me to do so. Really it is sad when we ladies get use to the Mr. Wrongs and settle. I shifted gears quickly; I must admit it took me a moment; mind you it took him time to get use to a young lady that was attractive and knew a lot of the street games, but was smart book wise also. The main attribute this man was attracted to, from what he shared with me down the river, was the good mother I was to my children. He never had natural children nor had been married. Oh my God I hit the jack pot!! Plus he never had a felony or criminal record. A squeaky clean record—what! Can this be real? Just remember, we all have our own personal issues and he had his. Our past can hinder our progress if we let it. Please don't let it. Deal with your pain, move on, and try not to beat yourself up from the poor choices you may have made. Go on and Live Well!! I remember Mr. Elder brought us one of the biggest most beautiful Christmas trees ever-- so large and tall that we had to cut the top off the tree to slide it in under the ceiling. Now of course we had to leave space for the star on top. My new guy did new gestures that were blowing my mind. By the way, the shell gas station we met at, there was and still is a well known restaurant across the street Kiss is it. You know the restaurant? My country guy treated me to dinner off the bat. He said, "You mean it is this late in the evening and you have not had dinner?" I got the complete soul food dinner—hey, he was paying for it. Back then, Le told me to be sure to get everything I wanted, Le is my husband now; see how things change? I did just that! I ordered chitterlings, Mac/cheese, collards, yams and cornbread, and peach cobbler. No shame in my game. I was chilling in his sharp Corvette, cruising without a bruising. This man let me break all of his rules on day one. He did have a no smoking sticker in his 'vette, I asked could I smoke, he said sure; of course I cracked the window. I also ended up spilling the chitterling juice in the clean sharp 'vette; he did not care, as I said he was crazy about your girl. Did you catch that? I felt bad about spilling the food because his car was so clean.

A different kind of guy took me to dinner and I hollered to my girl Tavia: "You got his license plate? Meet me at the crib in thirty minutes, if I am not there, call the police." My CG continued to show how gentle and kind he was to me and my daughters, Lord did I need what he had to offer. He still gives me the same sweet gentleness and kindness that reeled me in his arms, I am still happy in his arms twenty six years later. I asked God one day about this man. I said, "Lord, what did I do to deserve this man"? The Lord quickly replied, " I know what you have been through." When I asked God for the man I needed in my life, after being sick of the arguing and fighting with the street guys, local small level drug dealers, jail birds, and, even worse, possibly encountering men that were on the down low as well. I mean most of the men from around my neighborhood were constantly in and out of prison, they were not honest to themselves, and I surely didn't believe the bunk they would tell me. God had his hand on me. I am more than grateful that I had enough strength left to grab my future by the hand. Me and my new guy, we dated six years, and then he gave me the loveliest ring that I still wear, my engagement ring. So many women ooh and ahh about how pretty my ring is, and I always say, "I'd rather have the man any day than the ring and I'm more than blessed to have them both!" We have been together through it all: friendship, sickness, death of significant loved ones, love, raising children, purchasing real estate, education, building businesses together and relocating to Dallas TX and back to our home in Georgia together. So really it sounds like we have went 360 degrees.

As I would tell any young women, trust yourself, never let anyone tell you, you cannot have a dream and achieve that dream. Remember that you may have to change the things about yourself that may be hindering your growth. Whether it is your own dysfunction, the wrong type of guy, the crowd you may find yourself a part of, the environment, the lack of knowledge, power or resources. You have to tell others what you need and do your part to change your life for the better. No one wants a leech, and a person always crying, "why me?" I have started saying "why not me", I had to be stretched beyond the familiar pain I was accustomed to. Life has the answers we need but can we handle the answers? Trust God, learn to be vulnerable; I know this is not easy, especially when we have grown accustomed to acting like the super woman who can do it all, and probably have been at the point literally of emotionally hanging off the cliff. Life can bring you to a cliff at anytime in your walk for various reasons.

Please don't be a cliffhanger like I was, and sitting on the top of Fools Hill. Maybe look at the view that you are facing and make some positive choices; the main choice is always to live better with more inner peace. At times we are moving too fast and we are not even listening to our own selves. Slow that mustang down (smile). Really we have to pump the brakes and deep breathe. This book is dedicated to anyone and everyone who needs a lift in their spirit and who is not listening to God, momma, daddy, or that priceless friend in your ear. Take it from me I have been hungry, I have been homeless, proud and ignorant on top of it all. In addition I've wet my pillow many of nights because of desperation; while my girls slept I wept. Foolish pride put me out doors, when I could have lived the life of a princess if I had of stayed with Nana.

A hard head makes a soft (fill in the blank).

Mines made me a woman to be reckoned with. I had so much pain, and unsettled feelings because of life tossing me upside-down and then right side up. A girl from one of the poorest communities in upstate New York according to the history books and statistics, the Arbor Hill neighborhood from Albany, New York landed on her feet. Glory to God, I won the fight of my Life!

Time has its own clock. Here I am reflecting on about thirty years or so ago and to see how everything has changed-- not just changed but changed for the better because of determination and hard, hard work and never giving up!

Chapter 9

I CAN'T REMEMBER

My past had done a job on me as well as me feeding into unhealthy behaviors. As time continued to pass, I refused to be a prisoner of my childhood and the pain that consumed me. Deciding to be proactive, as I stated, I enrolled in GED classes, after the second try I passed the test. Yes! Next was RN school. Nursing was a passion for me, however the math associated with becoming a RN was a mountain, and this girl was not ready to climb. Tutors were an option and I had a couple of tutors; still I had such a fear of math that I continued to get in my own way. I moved on to another field of study: Hair. Yes I did exceptionally well in this field of study, I loved playing in the mirror, with makeup and hair, and surely looking pretty was all right up my alley. Still this was not enough. I went on to do facility contractual work, as I had dreamed and I made that dream materialize, because of my hard work. To this day, I am on my thirteenth facility of working with persons with Alzheimer's Disease; this has been the most rewarding thing ever as far as I am concerned, twenty one years in now, Can I say Wow? Yes I've stepped away from doing AD clients briefly and always found my way home. Back with those that can't remember who they are (let alone who I am), for some reason God laid this mission on my heart to beautify these people who were in their past very prominent people, at the top of their games, in their prime. Professionals, stay-at-home moms, doctor's, lawyer's, nurses, judges, therapists, teachers, custodians, life coaches and all other types of professionals from all walks of life and ethnicities. Alzheimer's is an illness that has taken so many millions by storm, not to mention the families, friends, and loved ones who have been blindsided because of the new member of the family that no one understands. Currently I am at the most advanced facility I have ever worked at, as far as the most advance stage of the disease; it is heart breaking! Some days I ask the Lord to help me and guide me as I deal with individuals who truly are depending on me and who need me to treat them as human beings. The families have helplessly watched in tears as the parent they used to know was robbed of their memory right before their very eyes.

Have you encountered anyone with AD? If so, I bet the conversation was pretty interesting. What I have learned to do is, embrace and meet them where they are at that particular moment. Typically the mind set will take the person back in their younger years, so I usually listen and maybe ask them questions about what they have just said to me. The answers are sometimes hilarious and memorable because they will say something out of left field in a normal voice and sometimes all I can do is hug them. Honestly I know my clients do not know my name but they do know my voice and they know I care; they also are very familiar with my hugs and the level of respect I feel is mandatory that they are worthy of. This disease is one of the most undignified, non-discriminating illnesses I have seen in some time. Some of the things I have seen from the clients, I will not share, for dignity purposes. Children of the parent's I have met are so touched by this illness and have shared with me the pain they feel, seeing the illness take its course. Some others can't deal with seeing their loved ones and refuse to visit, but they do continue to handle all financial and business matters. This bothers me, they still need us, I do feel deep in my heart of hearts that the person does reappear on occasions, and how dare my children or those that claim they love me give up on me? I can see how hard it may be; still it is already a lonely world, due to their memories are no longer operating at full capacity.

Sadly it may be barley functional; at that time is when they need us most. However I do commend those families that know I cannot do this, and they make the hard call to institutionalize the loved one. Some have asked me, "Nell, how can this Illness happen to such an amazing, wonderful, giving beautiful person?" I can't answer that. I see life as a Merry-Go-Round: if you get on this thing called life, where will you get off? When it's your turn, will you get off fully intact or what will grace bring our way? Will you be able to handle the blow that came straight out of left field and took you and yours by surprise? Or perhaps you're the mind reader that can predict the future. No one asks for this illness. Whatever the case, I'm prayerful my experiences, and sentiments will help someone else along the way who may be standing or walking in the AD storm right now. Over the past twenty-one years I have continually looked death in the eye and heard the last chain stroke breath far too often. When death gets so close, I know it when I see it coming in my folks, I now know the rhythms of the chest that I have witnessed far too often. I am reminded to thank them for their business and I share with them that I will miss them. Last but not least, I end the journey that the client and I have walked just like I started it: with a hug, but a farewell this time while praying they rest in peace.

When you walk through certain doors in life, race is no longer a factor. I've hugged many folks from every nationality being in these types of facilities. When it gets right down to it, all that matters is someone cares for another human being. My assignment called for love of a craft and the compensation followed right in line. Hurricane Katrina also sent a client my way displaced from the Big Easy, she landed in A.T.L. in a facility she was plagued with H.I.V from a cheating husband who tried Viagra and took to the street for sex, he contracted the illness and brought it home to his wife of many years. Looking at that senior, I would say to myself, "She looks so mean all the time," until I heard her story. Down the line I saw a smile. She had the most beautiful hair: wavy, soft, pretty and grey-streaked. They had been married for many years. She lost out on a lot of levels coming from what appeared to be the Purple River ride in her life. As I walked this journey, I found out that, whether we are young or old we all have a story and we all want to tell it to the right person. Not to be judged, simply to be heard, understood, and uninterrupted. Everyone may not deserve to hear some of the most intimate details of our pain, strengths, or triumphs. God had me on assignment, I'm shifting, and drifting on this Purple River as he speaks to my heart and directs my landings.

Please take time to review the (10) warning signs of Alzheimer's:

- Memory loss that disrupts daily life
- Challenges in planning or solving problems
- Difficulty completing familiar tasks at home, at work or at leisure
- Confusion with time or place
- Trouble understanding visual images and spatial relationships
- New problems with words in speaking or writing
- Misplacing things and losing the ability to retrace steps
- Decreased or poor judgment
- Withdrawal from work or social activities
- Changes in mood and personality

What to do if you notice these signs

If you notice any of the 10 Warning Signs of Alzheimer's in yourself or someone you know, don't ignore them. Schedule an appointment with your doctor.

With early detection, you can:

Get the maximum benefit from available treatments —You can explore treatments that may provide some relief of symptoms and help you maintain a level of independence longer. You may also increase your chances of participating in clinical drug trials that help advance research. God Bless!

The referenced data on Alzheimer's can be found at http://www.alz.org/alzheimers_disease_10_signs_of_alzheimers.asp
My journey has not been easy with this clientele base, however I would not trade it I feel this was my God given assignment for his purpose.

Chapter 10

RIDING THE REAL ESTATE WAVE

There are those who relate to living outside of the box; I am one of those people. I knew early on that the regular nine to five was not for me, but you must crawl prior to walking and I did just that. Once we passed the initial pre-licensing for appraiser's exam. We were thrilled; now we had to find a mentor to teach us this highly skilled trade, which I had not heard of. Passing that first test was only the beginning of this unpredictable ride into the unknown. One day in spring, I was out enjoying the weather with my husband, searching for real estate, when I ran across a man working. He had a clip board, shorts, and a polo top. He looked to me to have the best job ever. Me being nosey, I asked him what he was doing and what his title was. He shared some information with me and I was hooked on the thought of making hunks of money with no boss breathing down my neck, plus my freedom. I pursued the position; my hubby wanted to become a home inspector, so I said we can both do both professions. Yes, we had some serious studying in front of us; we did it though. Not only did we become appraisers and home inspectors, we also achieved our business degrees together. Yup, me and my CG (country guy).

We are still making positive history together. So again I ask you to never let another tell you what you can't do; and what is even worse than them telling you, you can't do something is when they constantly say they can't believe you are doing so well, possibly a little better than they expected. I am just saying set your own limits because your haters have already done so. I thank a former talk show host for saying years and years ago, "Don't get mad at people, just live well." Once you start living so well, your haters no longer matter; that is a great place and I'm there. Okay, just so that we are clear, it has nothing to do with the world on the outside of me; it all has to do with my inner core of owning my value as a person. The Purple River inside of me had many potholes, dead end signs, mountains, valley experiences and disappointments along my way, and I made a few U-turns. However, as I crossed bridges, I did my best not to burn my bridges and, If I did, I made my way back at least to say I'm sorry and asked for forgiveness. There is nothing wrong with saying I'm sorry. I went ahead and freed myself from internal torture that others will happily pass on to you because of their own misery. Please don't except their madness! Realize it is a job getting to a place of peace and freedom and staying there. Life is all about the choices we make. If you have the time, sleep on a big decision first and of course pray about all things, big and small, without ceasing, and then decide. More than the aforementioned suggestions also consult with a person you look up to and trust.

Moving on; we had to find mentorship; this was a real task because of the lack of mentors with affordable fees for the internship. A neighbor who lives in our community was able to help us find mentorship. We found a brilliant man who taught us the craft-- I am not going to go knee-deep and tell you the crazy stuff we went through, as we learned what I will call the "appraiser's office from, you fill in the blank ". Just put it this way: when we graduated, we were computer techs from fixing the tacky outdated computers, and pest control people from killing the big roaches and mice. Surely after this long season in our life of dealing with the manner in which our mentor ran his establishment, needless to say we were also experts in people skills, and we learned patience, specifically how not to cuss out our boss. You talk about being on fire after waiting weeks or months for our measly paychecks.

All I could do was pray constantly that one of us would pass the State exam and we would be able to get out of the madness, we found ourselves in the midst of. Any associates from that era who may read this book will either laugh or cry because they know it is the gospel. When I tell you it was nothing nice, please believe it! Now came time for us to ask someone for help in the appraiser's office, where we are the new kids on the block. So the seasoned appraiser's were just looking at us, seemingly mad because we are husband and wife, and that meant automatically we would make double the money. Someone pinch me for the madness I signed up for and did not have a clue about! Or maybe I am just fussing with myself for being in a ghetto fabulous appraiser's office? I'm not sure that you will believe what I am getting ready to tell you next: I thank the Lord for the training we got from this same place that I could not stand. As time passed and I looked back on the hard lessons we learned in the appraiser's office, I now laugh and thank God for keeping us strong through such a trying time on our path to success! Our mentor passed away a year ago on July 4th 2014. I will always thank him in my heart for, as he said, for "Teaching Us How to Fish," meaning he taught us how to survive. He taught us the old school, hard way, and because of Walter we are some of the crème of the crop appraisers. Another one of his trainees is the vice president of Bank of America, so you do the math. That place I described as ghetto fabulous payed off big for over the hundreds of black appraisers who were trained under this brilliant black professional's watch. Thank you Walter, I love and miss you.

May you rest in peace my friend and mentor. I have to say what's up to my girl, Ms. Dor, the office manager in the appraiser's office. She is still my girl!! When I need a great reference, she always has my back, a true original. We still have fun and get together when we can, on special occasions. We were getting our feet wet with this new trade and making excellent money, and seeing the state of Georgia together and loving it! Years passed. Then we started hearing of the real estate market that would bust soon. Well it happened, the market crashed and so did we. Our lives crashed and smashed with it. It was terrible! So many real estate professionals out of work, foreclosures everywhere, all the baller's Broke, what? Folks, with PHD are working at Mickey D's?

Other appraisers committing suicide in other states, due to being broke and losing everything. We were facing foreclosure ourselves and had reached our breaking point with the bank. The banks were very overwhelmed from so many folk just walking away from their homes. Some people were setting fires for insurance money and doing whatever they could do to stay afloat. Many of my counterparts are in prison now and many others have their professional licenses revoked, while other just surrendered their licenses. The Great Recession was Horrible! Thankfully we are multi-talented, shifting gears doing odd jobs and making ends meet any way possible; I am thankful for help from our families and God's Grace got us through. The season we were faced with in our lives was humbling for sure. These are some of the shifts that life will bring you to on the Purple River ride in life, where you feel as if you are about to capsize! Instead you may just drift awhile, check out the currants and the waves up or down the stream.

Does anyone feel where I am going? I am sharing how life will take you places beyond your control, but you have to ride, stand or fall. None of the valley experiences I had made me a loser, however I was called a loser by many. But these challenges, they all made me stronger due to me constantly investing in myself. Continuing on my journey, I was equipped with endurance and determination to succeed. Yes, I did get weak; I cried and felt sorry for myself. I also wanted to throw in the towel more than you know. Just think if I had of quit though; I never would have written my first book.

Follow me on the Purple River, please stay the course and trust God, surround yourself with good people, hold your head up and keep the faith! My river ride took me North, South, East and West and sadly sometimes we didn't know what to do next, although, we ended up going West this next time. We took our broke biscuit's to a new frontier: Dallas, Texas. North Dallas is where we lived and called home for six months, to be exact. I felt like I was on the ride of my life again in a new place, totally distraught from leaving the life we worked so hard to build, missing my family while they were missing us too! A husband upset with me from saying I have to try something other than waiting for the Marshall's to come and evict us for nonpayment of the mortgage. We did not have any sound source of income. I'm sure you know the saying, "when your income is less than your overhead, then your outcome will be your down fall." Hey, I did get my first corporate position also in Texas; I was blessed to get a good job with the Dallas County Schools system, too. The girl from the mean streets of Albany, New York, did not do badly for herself, with the CG by her side.

He was not as blessed in the job department in Texas; however, he did have work. So every little bit did count. I would sit in my husband's truck and cry everyday on my lunch break. While I had the big time corporate job-- the same job I swore if I just got I will be set!--the money was no longer the most important factor. I hated the fake corporate atmosphere and the job period. I stayed at the corporate position for a month and a day, and then resigned. Time away from Decatur, GA gave me time to finish up my degree in business and contemplate on our lives. The beautiful brick house was still ours in GA. We were trying to do a short sale for it with the bank. Gratefully, being that the home had not sold yet, within the six months we were gone. We made the decision to return back to our roots and give it another try. Yes we packed up and drove back home. The bank had a great new program in place, because they had messed up so many families and it was a big mess. The program the banks had could only help if we were still residing in our home. We were distraught to say the least, thinking of how we were traveling back and forth. Deciding to go back home, we packed up, heading for Decatur once again. Glory to God, it had been a true blessing in disguise. One thing about starting from the nub is, you learn from the ground up. A scary time, because the unemployment rate was in the double digits and hitting historical lows, so that meant crime was skyrocketing.

Guess what? God kept us, won't he do it? My voice was silent for years as a child, feeling as though, I was in a world without my own power back then. Over time a beautiful rainbow emerged through all of my storms & thoughts. Some people advised others not to look back on their painful past, but it is vital to reflect on your past and see how you made it through that trying season. Grandma said "Never forget where you come from" all of the less than perfect men, bad decisions, being given away as a child and becoming a mother as a teenager was all part of who I was, my pain and my God-- given plan as well. Regardless of what we think, when we lean on our own understanding, we may confuse ourselves. God will always guide and provide. I dare you to trust him. Try him for yourself, please.

Chapter 11

REAL VOICES OF INSPIRATION & PAIN

Here are words of wisdom quoted from a Nursing professional of more than fifty years, who was also one of the hands of love that cared for me as a child and continues to be a support beam. I am the daughter she did not have and she was the mother I so needed:

"Unfortunates learn from their mistakes, and the lucky ones learn from others mistakes."-- **Joyce Robinson.**

This next entry is from the mouth of babes, my niece. A young lady who is in the eighth grade shares her inspiration in a short but powerful message—Oh, Happy 13th Birthday Miss Raven! I was there the day you were born and the day your parents got married. You are still as beautiful today as the first day you came into this world. I am very proud of you and my nephew. Kisses:

"Never let your hard times come between your good times."—Raven

Since this next young lady was transparent enough to share her feelings, I want to thank you --Ms. Neva Cook, for our meeting. And for such a heartfelt conversation with a young lady who was in foster care and unfortunately has spent time in the judicial system, in Missouri and Georgia. When I looked in your eyes and heard some of your testimonies, all I can say is "I'm that girl" you are so intelligent, beautiful, and funny. Be certain to forgive first for yourself; and then for those who have hurt you. Lift the concrete blocks off your heart, toss them aside and grace the world with your wisdom and knowledge that comes from your pain as you continue to heal and live well. Miss Neva, you are a lovely budding flower who is waiting for the Springtime river ride to show your true beauty, speak love, health, wealth and joy into your future, while placing the past pain in its rightful place within your soul. Here is her submission:

"I didn't grow up in the system. At a few points of my young childhood I had my mother and my father. Things at one point were actually what many would call 'normal'. The thing is, though, I am not a rookie to the system. At the age of eight, I was placed in the Missouri Foster Care system. Being that I was only eight, I didn't really understand why things were happening to me. Actually, all I wanted was to return home with my family. And at the age of ten, I was granted that privilege, which I didn't regret, until I began to understand why certain things happened to me.

When I was fourteen, I re-entered the system in a new state- Georgia to be exact. And at the beginning, I felt the same way I did as an eight- year-old kid. The only thing that changed my outlook on my situation was the treatment I received by the main culprit, my father. As a child, he always treated me as this 'special child'; even though I was not allowed to be called a princess, this is what I was treated like. As a blooming teenager, things changed and my father became this evil being whom I couldn't have controlling me any longer. As I have grown up, I don't feel as oblivious as I did as that eight-year old child in Missouri's system. I feel as If I have bloomed into a young blossom that is still in need of some self-searching. A lot of people feel as if the kids who are unfortunately placed within the system are nothing but strains on society. But we as Americans fail to understand that we all have our own stories, whether we are born into wealth or are forced into a life of uncertainty. As a young woman, I have realized that no matter who is in my corner to cheer me on, I have to push myself first. That is why I don't fret about not having my mother and father. That is why I don't fret about having family in general to cheer me on. Because no matter what I or anyone else in this matter chooses to pursue in their life, it is up to us to make the needed decisions to get to where we need to be. And that no matter what, as long as the correct path is taken, the right crowd will assist from all over."-- Ms. Neva Cook

All I can say is "Amen". Furthermore I want to Congratulate Ms. Neva as she did graduate from high school recently and in enrolled in West Georgia College. In spite of the personal challenges she faced on her Purple River ride through life. When

I say, "I'm that girl", I am referring to the pain of going through being shifted and uprooted, as well as being with someone that truly cares and because of immaturity, we rejected the genuine love from the hand that is there to help us heal. Yet later we look back and realize how priceless that person or those people were on our journeys to becoming women. The feelings of traumatic despair can be overwhelming to say the least, I have been there.

(Go Neva! Keep your head up! You will always be my sister, girl!)

Moreover, I would like to say to Ms. D, a foster mother to this young lady, you are heaven-sent to the children who find themselves within these governmental systems for extending the unselfish time, love quality of life, and dignity to the youth that land on your doorstep and in your heart. I have seen how you spare no expenses when it comes to the children you care for; they all look more than cared for. I love you for caring. You have gone above and beyond the state's call of duty.

Thank you for sharing and connecting spiritually with me as we do our morning water aerobics at the YWCA. You are a blessing to the kids and the world! May God have a Royal Purple place in Heaven just for you, for your deeds done on this earth with the children caught in the trenches of life and governmental systems due to their family issues.

The last entry is from a young lady that has a few Best Sellers in her soul I'm certain. I have watched this young lady carry the storms of life and she still stands. We will not share every aspect of her life out of respect and, personally, I feel every detail of one's life is not meant to be shared with the world. Again all the above referenced people were kind enough and honest enough to share from their hearts words of inspiration and encouragement to help young women and all women along with the men in our worlds. Oftentimes we may find ourselves depressed or in painful places and wonder, "How did I get here and what do I do to get to a better place, mentally, financially, physically and emotionally?" Claim you place in the world, never let anyone tell you, you don't deserve love, peace or happiness. Moreover how dare a person try to keep you tied to your past? We all have a past, just keeping it real.

Sometimes you just have to "snatch it"—that is to say, take what is yours when you have done your due diligence, left skin in the game, worked, and done all that was necessary to get to a better place. You no longer made excuses of why you couldn't do it. You asked for what your soul desired and you trusted God and stood on his promise. Moving forward, most of us have learned valuable lessons that turned out to be priceless. In my book, I have not used any big fancy words. I choose to keep my message clear to all. I'm praying the passion I have in my heart will be felt within the pages of this book written to give back, inspire, motivate, encourage, or heal another heart in or out of a lifestorm. Yes, this is my first literary project and may be my favorite piece, as time goes on when I reflect. It was scary to get started but it also felt natural as I opened my honest heart, not to bash, disrespect or conceal my emotions. Once I began connecting with like spirits, honest women and young ladies that have a heart as I do, I knew without a doubt I had to share my story and experiences in hopes of guiding others to make wiser choices with life-changing decisions and to live well beyond their personal pain, regardless of where the pain came from. Use your past as the gas you may need to stay inspired as you keep it moving! We as women have worn umbrellas, makeup, and smiles for centuries to cover up our pain. I don't know about you but my pain went "grave deep" as my Grandma would say, meaning, I will take certain things to my grave with me. However I still stand, smile, embrace, respect, listen, live, learn and grow from pain, love, and indifferences and now know I am not suppose to walk through every door, stand on every stage, in all audiences or cry because everybody else does.

My heart belongs to me and God has set me free to continue my ride along the Purple River as it connects to the amazing oceans and to the Glorious Sea.

Families Apart

True inside beauty will shine strong at the darkest in your family life. Most families will experience dark moments in their families' lives at some point and time. However, we must allow the inner beauty to shine through it all. Many families are apart for many reasons: Jail, off to War for their country, long hours on the job, mental illness, one half of the family lives in one state or country, and/or death. I strongly encourage families to be strong and allow their beauty to shine brightly through it all. Get up get and get dressed, each and every day, and start to repair and /or fill in the gap of their loved ones. Life was never supposed to be easy. Life was designed to have issues that you must overcome. If we stay down and out, everything and everybody around us will get down and out also.

However, there are many people out there in this world who, no matter what may take place in or around them, they will continue to shine brightly no matter what life brings their way. Keep smiling!

Many will put pressure on individuals around them, due to the fact they are missing their loved one. Many times individuals will turn to drinking and drugs to fill in the pain of their loved ones. And that is not good whatsoever. Individuals should take time out to love themselves and respect each other. Being apart from your loved one is a part of life, even though we may not agree with it. However it will be kind to support and deal with the time apart with grace. Finally, in due time all families around the world will be reunited once and for all. Everyone will be happy eating food, dancing, and smiling as a happy family. Just be patient and everything will be alright. -- Shatika L. Johnson

Chapter 12

DREAM YOUR BIGGEST DREAM

This chapter is a dedicated to all young ladies that have went through tough times and landed on your feet. I salute you, and love you; I ask that you continue to love yourselves in spite of what your circumstances look like today or what you may have gone through. You have to know better, to want better, to see better, to be better, and do better to live better. I challenge you to keep your self-esteem up; dream your biggest dream and chase it, until you have gone your furthest and watch God do the rest. It never ever fails; if it is meant for you, it's yours. Be sure that you don't get in your own way. Think healthy.

Reach out to me any time. I do appreciate you picking up my book "Purple River". My hopes are that you have read a young girls story that loves the color Purple and has been through a wealth of experiences as wide as a River and deep as the sea. She proudly wears a crown of victory, landed in the hearts of angels. She took to the mean streets of Upstate Albany, New York-in The Arbor Hill Community. Everyone does not make it out to tell their story; God is using me. I hope that you walked along side my emotional journey and saw the growth and transparency in between the lines of my life on the Purple River. I eventually saw the beauty in the storm on down the river. Keep walking tall, never allowing another to make you feel small or less than you are, which is wonderfully and perfectly made! Make yourself proud! You have to first own what you want before you can give it to another. No matter what it may be from the following wisdom, love, respect, honesty, integrity, friendship, joy, or peace, I WISH YOU ALL OF THESE. Because I am a Victor-- this happens to be my father's name-- I now have the victory as well as, I have the love and respect of my father, and he has mine. No one is perfect. I forgive my father for his absence; more than that, he is the only dad I will ever have and I Love him!

Chapter 13

PURPLE RIVER FINDS THE SEA & LIVES WELL

The uncertainties I felt from living in the midst of a storm, with a mother that had her own mental issues, and a dad that was in the middle of living his life on his terms. Yes I needed them both and I will always have a place of sorrow deep place within myself for the child that deserved so much more (simply, she deserved her parents). There is no reason for me to carry anger, for the end results typically is death or regrets. Nevertheless I can now spend quality time with some of the main people in my life that initiated the deepest pains of my childhood. Amazingly I have now conquered feelings that were overwhelmingly destructive and consuming mentally, during my young life. Living well is the best blessing ever! I landed in a place just for me, my own space in the world that I call home. The lady who raised me, Nana, is a street named after my Nana Margarette Drive, which I used daily to get home. The street I reside on is her sister's name. I am happy to be where I finally ended up, in safe arms at last with my husband. I am no longer a slave driver working like a crazy woman, for my body won't allow it anymore. Confused as to: where do I belong; who likes or loves me; are these people really my friends; what if my car, house, man, or money does not compare to anyone else's standards but mine? God has set me free from all of the foolishness I once thought made me or would break me. Honestly I don't know when the burden was lifted, but God knew I needed the internal rest. One of my daily prayers was and still is: I asked God to "Set me free from all the things that are not like Him."

My peace is wonderful, especially knowing that the world did not give me this peace, and as I heard Pastor Smith say in church, and the world can't take it away. I've reiterated several times throughout my book how we can't allow another to take the steering wheel of our destiny. You have to learn to drive and stay in your lane in life. Do your best to avoid "self-inflicted wounds" meaning poor choices. When you make poor choices, you may lose your peace, your power, or your freedom on one level or another. My passion does not stop with the words on the pages of this book. I would love to connect and speak with you if necessary to help, give back, inspire, motivate and encourage you to live well. My heart is at rest with my life now. I would also like to apologize to anyone and everyone whom I may have needed to say I'm sorry to and was unaware that I hurt in some form or fashion. Life is about owning what's yours and being set free from the birdcage of life. After my ride on the "Purple River" in fact I drifted right into the sea called life. I now know what my assignment is in life, and I will share that in my next book. Realize our assignments may change at any time along the journey called life to help ourselves & others. Real life is unscripted!

The End

And the rest and best of my life Begins~

CLOSING REMARKS

My book was written to help someone along the way: Possibly through growing pains, a new business, young love, childhood struggles, health challenges(mentally or emotionally), or maybe simply to find the ultimate love between, me, myself and I (and my CG). Because surely, we cannot give away or share that of which we don't own yet ourselves. The power and humbleness to be vulnerable, Love, respect, forgiveness, confidence and being transparent enough to know it may not always be something wrong with everyone else but ourselves. Own your mess period, and then move on to the clear path called a "reasonably happy life". Between these lines were years of pain that I experienced coming into this day , where I am now a mature woman who can understand how life takes you to unexpected sometime dark places, painful lonely walks, and tumultuous rides and shifts in our hearts along the river called life. Sometime we cannot always explain what and why seasons happened.

Whatever the case may be, I wanted to touch a heart somewhere or everywhere, one that somehow knows and understands some of what I was feeling growing up, unwanted from the door of life. Someone just shared with me today August 8, 2015, that her niece did take her own life due to the pain of not having her mother in her life and from the pains of her childhood that were never resolved. This is real. Many of us out here in the world are hurting, men and women, and we need help. My spirit was shattered at a young age. I thought the gap in my teeth was ugly until I was reassured that this identified my beautiful uniqueness.

Life lessons took me places that were predestined for my growth and anointing. I was perfectly made to be the special individual that would raise two amazing young, beautiful ladies on my own. For a long season, I relocated to new frontier more than a couple of times in my life and went on to become a professional woman that can and does wear multiple professional hats. As a real property appraiser, home inspector, medical secretary, Business graduate, Community HOA president that was awarded a Proclamation and Vice President (twice), I have adopted and personally cleaned a road in my community for more than ten years and counting. I am a mobile notary and a master Cosmetologist with thirteen facilities in my twenty-one year stretch of doing hair for person's with Alzheimer Disease and other types of health challenges. At one point in my career, it was laid on my heart to provide professional salon services for a Behavioral Children's Hospital, of which there were 103 kids there when I had the contract as the Master Cosmetologist. I understood some of the internal pain these children felt because I was that child, feeling like I was unwanted and unloved for many years by the people I needed to love me. I lost my self esteem, until I got it together and continued to walk with my head up and came out of my pity party and took back what was mine, a right to the tree called life. You can do it too!

A true life that consisted of, education, hard work, on the job training, going back to get my GED, (due to my dropping out of school in the tenth grade), and leaving the drugs alone, I also became a home owner, and I went back to school with my husband by my side and now we both hold Business Degrees.

This same young girl from a low economic environment, hungry many days and nights as a child, abused and tossed away made it out! She came out on the winning side in every single category she faced as a child, girl, and then as a young lady. Now released and set free from the mental and emotional bondage that I wore like a piece of clothing. My prayers are that the dads, husbands: brothers, uncles, friends, granddads and mentors will all see the vitality of their presence in our lives as women. To the men that have remained in the lives of their daughters/wives, personally I thank you! This is not intended to bash or disrespect any man.
I am simply sharing my personal feelings and those of many, many girls and women whom I have spoken with, and connected with throughout my journey. Although it is never too late to step

in and stay a part of the picture called her life as long as you both have breath, life, and the desire for a relationship. Regardless we need our men to own up and step up to the plate and make that lifelong commitment to stand and stay. Our dads are supposed to be our hero's. We have to stop trying to carry life on our backs alone. Tell the man in your heart how important and precious he is in your life. Our men have feelings too. Every person wants to feel needed. For the men that have step up and guided another in a positive light, you will be blessed, and Thank you for the love and unselfishness! Karma is real. The universe has its own way of giving us what we deserve in God's speed.

Remember this girl; she was not going to be a success by many accounts. You must keep in mind that all of mankind have imperfections and have fallen short. I'm sure the same people, who were your biggest critics, have fallen short as well, somehow, in their walk; don't believe they haven't. We all must first fall to stand tall for our call.

I did it!! Deciding I wanted better and I did better, I had much help along the way, Spiritual love, sisterly love, brotherly love, good love, and bad love, which I needed to help me see the difference between the two. Additionally I received financial support, emotional support, and Community support. Physiological support from counseling, welfare support, governmental support and family support were all necessities and vital on my ride to first loving myself and then on for me to be able to receive love from a man that was ready to dig deep and stay until death do us part as our vows stated. Some people actually may not see the benefit(s) of professional counseling. Well I am a cheerleader all the way for healing yourself from the inside out with professional help. Counseling can be the best gift you ever give yourself to enable yourself to live your best life now!! Most importantly I want to thank the father's of my God-given daughters; life was extremely difficult as a single mother living in Albany and Georgia.

Because I never stopped trying, God met me at every stop sign and every detour when I wanted to give up. My children have been blessings in my life, hands down. Even though I am not with the fathers of my children, the seasons of my life with those men were the worse in my life. The best thing I have ever done was to leave those men. I grew from the pains I learned to trust, from being with Mr. Wrongs. In that hurricane season of my life on the Purple River, I clearly saw how much I didn't understand about life, love, men or dysfunction. So I've learned to love myself more and grew to expect better treatment from men, and from anyone in my personal circle for that fact. Cherish, your beauty on the inside first, then the outside. One thing about inner beauty: it last forever. Always use common sense. I've seen common sense get people in doors that money or degrees could not. Be wise, ladies!

Time has a way of healing, concealing and revealing all things. Spend your time living on purpose instead of stressing over irrelevant things. You choose your battles in life with caution; what seems like a mountain today may minimize in size or importance tomorrow. Life can be funny yet serious, and too precious to waste.

Pray about EVERYTHING! Keep a positive cheering section in your life; joy comes in the morning!!!

Please, please keep walking and don't be too hard on yourselves. I seriously feel as if I can't stress the aforementioned sentence enough! You can and will make it. If you feel the need to glance back on your past, it is okay. Because only then can you measure your success! We have to look at where we started and if it was a fair race to start with. In spite of it all, I pray that something I've shared or others have shared within this book will help you see a brighter day is around the corner. Maybe something in the next book, church service, phone call, letter, breath, conversation, dream, e-mail or text may have a break through message for you.

God does move in mysterious ways. Keep your head up and believe in yourself, not your circumstances. Everyone has a book in side of them; many folk in my circle were happy to hear I was finally writing my book. Maybe I will keep this writing thing up? I will see. The book sales will let me know if you want more of me. Hahaha. We all have stories of triumph and testimonies. Believe that your journey is not by mistake. We are all being pruned and prepped for what's next, for our God-given assignments; you have to keep living to find out what your God-given assignment is. Wherever you may find yourself at this very moment as you read Purple River, if it is not where you want to be, keep it moving until you put your hands and heart on your dream! Additionally, if by chance you are staring adversity in the face once more, do some true soul searching and climb that mountain, until you find the star that you are inside your real beauty. Hold it up and say, "I made it, and I learned lessons of a life time on the Purple River." You are not alone in this; it does take a village to live, love, and to last! By the way, you can call this lady Purple

I love you and Thank you

ABOUT THE AUTHOR

Annelle Johnson Elder ~ Yes! I have now conquered my hardest hurdles from my childhood. I am a wife, mother of two gorgeous adult daughters, two amazing and intelligent grandchildren, and a grand pet Yorkie, Jax. For Many years I have served my community in various capacities as listed below:

The HOA President, Vice President, Community Spokesperson, Senior Advocate, Community Safety Liaison and served on the welcoming committee. My husband and I are both appraisers & home inspectors and we've had a small real estate company for nearly fifteen years. Additionally I've held a Master Cosmetology license for twenty one years in the State of Georgia. While working as a Nursing Assistant years ago, I was drawn to helping and enjoying the Elderly residents that were my patients and now are my clients. At that time, not realizing exactly what Alzheimer's was, I learned of it quickly. Instantly I had compassion for this clientele base and as I looked back, I wonder where has the time gone? I have been providing professional human services (Beauty Services) and love to this community of clients for more than Twenty two years. When my children were small I worked as a medical secretary, in a hospital for nearly ten years and ultimately went on to further my education. Together my husband and I achieved our Business Degree's in 2011. The girls are now grown and on their own. Realizing, I am still not finished with embarking on my creative talents. I decided to write my Inspirational Autobiography with hopes of sharing, giving back, and being as transparent as possible, with hopes of saving a young lady from making poor choices that may stunt her growth down the river ride in life. Also for the mature women that still find themselves emotionally in upside-down situations from time to time. And a heartfelt message for any dad or husband out there that finds it hard to understand the emotional rollercoaster Purple River ride that women are on, from the baggage that is ours and some that is passed on: We need you to stay and love us unconditionally. Let's get healthy together.

I was determination to excel in life; I came out on the Winning side from all of the personal hurdles I faced. See them listed below: I did the work!

Depression, Rebellion

Domestic Abuse

Low Self-Esteem,

Abandonment Issues

Chemical Dependency

Homelessness

Being a Single Teenage Mom

Picking Mr. Wrong's

High School Dropout

Divorce at a young age

Being on Welfare/Section 8

Relocated Twice for a Better Life

Read how I turned the positive corners and lived a great life after a lot of hard work. I got it together! You can do it Too!

Please feel free to contact me with questions on Speaking Engagements and Bulk Book Order's via any of the avenues listed below:

Annelle Johnson Elder:
Dba: Purple River books Enterprise LLC
4567 Rockbridge Rd. #1771 Pine Lake, GA 30072
Email: purpleriverbooks@gmail.com
Website: www.purpleriverbooksenterprise.com
Phone: 404-274-1480
Fax: 404-855-5127

"Live Well"